KINGDOM

Girl, GET YOUR FIGHT BACK

A NEXT LEVEL SHIFT
VOLUME 3

KINGDOM MINDED WOMEN DECLARING
ITS YOUR WINNING SEASON!

TRINA D. WELLS

Copyright © Trina D. Wells, 2018

All rights reserved. No part of this book may be reproduced in any form without permission in writing from the author. Reviewers may quote brief passages in reviews.

DISCLAIMER

No part of this publication may be reproduced or transmitted in any form or by any means, mechanical or electronic, including photocopying or recording, or by any information storage and retrieval system, or transmitted by email without permission in writing from the author.

Neither the author nor the publisher assumes any responsibility for errors, omissions, or contrary interpretations of the subject matter herein. Any perceived slight of any individual or organization is purely unintentional.

Brand and product names are trademarks or registered trademarks of their respective owners.

Contents

Preface   5

SaTina Grissom   7
A Beautiful ~~Waste~~ WAIT   7

Casonya Carter   15
My Genesis "I'm Living a New Life"   15

Shawanda Tumblin   25
I HAVE SINNED NOW WHERE DO I GO FROM HERE? LORD, I'M NOT WORTHY OF YOUR GRACE   25

Anna L. Crockett   33
Girl Get Your Fight Back -Piece by Piece   33

Carolyn O'Bryant   41
I am a Survivor not a Victim   41

Dr. Cynthia J. Hines   49
PUT A NAME ON IT   49

Shonquil "Shonny" Jones Dyson   59
The Setback That Became the Setup   59

JacQuaye A. Payne   67
"I Am One Person" Fight For Your Right To Be You   67

Denise Harris   77
Lady in the Pew   77

Angela R. Flowers   85
AS THE SHIFT BEGAN   85

Sherry Johnson   95
It's Me and My Story   95

Sherice Dixon   103
THE FIGHT IS FIXED   103

Kmetris Hunt   109
Let 'YOU' Arise   109

Pamela Buford   117
Girl, Get Your Fight Back Poem Collection   117

Preface

Welcome to Spiritual Bootcamp,

GGYFB will prepare you for the battle ahead as you engage in spiritual confrontation with the enemy. You will learn how to fight the good fight of faith from fourteen of our Next Level Authors that will empower you to advance your life to the Next Level. There is an invisible war going on, whether you choose to acknowledge it or not. The war begins in the heavenly but the battlefield in your mind. (2 Corinthians 10:4)

The bible gives numerous accounts of how Jesus counter-attacked Satan attacks against Him. Jesus was a Skilled Warrior, therefore, He sought His Heavenly Father for strategies on how to apply the rules of engagement against Satan. Fortunately, we have been given the same heavenly access, knowledge, power and kingdom authority to counter-attack every attack sent to devour our purpose, spiritual identity, assignment and kingdom destiny. Jesus is our example, therefore we must follow His instructions as we are led into our Winning Season!

The enemy is aware of our rich inheritance in Christ Jesus which is why he works endlessly hours against us with hopes of wearing us down so low that we will eventually give up and surrender our lives to him. Do not quit, it is time to walk in our kingdom authority and possess our land. Although, you may be weary, the Bible instructs us not too, "Be not weary in well-doing, for in due season you will reap if you faint not." (Gal 6:9) We are born winners, and each one of us have a "due season "coming. Therefore, we must remain strong in the Lord, in the power of His might if we expect to walk in

Total Victory. (Eph 6: 10) The enemy will never fight fair, he prepares for the "knock out" but as we learn how he use his weapons against our spiritual eyes will become open to see that the one whose fighting against us is no greater than the one fighting for us. (John 10:10)

You may look like you are surrounded but in actuality you are surrounded by Him/Jesus! Therefore, it is possible to win ever battle set before us but we must constantly take on the mind of Christ and stop counting our losses and start counting our wins. We Were Born Winners!

#GGYFB
Trina D. Wells

SaTina Grissom

A BEAUTIFUL ~~WASTE~~ WAIT

"You are a Beautiful Waste."

"Excuse Me?"

"You're a Beautiful Waste. You are beautiful on the outside, but you've made some really bad

decisions that have caused your life to be a waste."

"WOW!!! Is that how you see me? "

"Yup!"

What was I to say behind that? God, am I a waste? God, how can I possibly be the apple of your eye, when someone else sees me as a Beautiful Waste? Maybe they see something in me that I don't see in myself?

"A Beautiful Waste." Those words repeated themselves over in my mind more times than I chose to count. The more I tried to block out the word snares of yet another individual, the more my inner woman was at an all- time low.

"WHATEVER! I'M GOOD WITH ME...AND WHOEVER DOESN'T LIKE ME NEED TO CONSULT GOD! I'M TIRED OF PEOPLE THINKING THEY HAVE THE RIGHT TO SPEAK THEIR HEARTS DESIRES WHEN IT COMES TO ME!"

"Sticks and stones may break my bones, but words will NEVER hurt me!" (Sticking my tongue out like I'm a little kid on the playground.) Wait a minute! Who was the heartless, Tin-Man individual that came up with that stupid poem? Words do hurt, and who was I fooling? I sure wasn't fooling myself. I was hurt to the core of my heart. I was tore up, from the floor up...in the words of my mentor I was, "THUH." Those words penetrated my heart like someone had sucker punched me the stomach. "A WASTE, A WASTE, A WASTE." I tried to downplay the words in my mind, but to no avail; there they remained. Repeating itself loudly as if it was being announced over a loud speaker; "Clean up in aisle three, IT'S A WASTE!"

I needed someone to minister to me. I needed someone to speak life into what I heard as a death sentence. "God, I need you to send someone to reaffirm me, because right now I'm not sure who or what I am. I don't know if I'm a waste or the apple of your eye." I needed my soul ministered to.

A BEAUTIFUL WAIT
(...and it was Good)

God knows who to send to speak in your life just when you need it most. He always has a ram inthe bush. God directed me to my cousin, Kay. As I was sharing with her the scenario of the conversation, she said in the most calming voice, "Tina I didn't hear God say, A Beautiful Waste, but I did hear him say, a Beautiful Wait ."

First of all, the devil knows who to use to hurt us the most. Secondly, he blinds the spiritual sight of people. They never see the things of God or the transformation that is or has taken place in ones life. Spiritually blinded individuals are always focused on the negatives of what was and what used to be; versus the what is or what will be. You are a Beautiful Wait . Nothing, and I do mean absolutely nothing, that God ever created was a waste. In the book of Genesis chapter 7, every time God added a new element to his creation and finished a project he said, "And it was Good." Tina, God had you included in that statement, you are good. You were on his mind long before the foundation of the world began.

God has already taken you through many pains of life. You are now going through the process, which is a part of your purpose. The pain, the process and the purpose is all a part of whom you are becoming and who God created you to be. God is doing a new thing in you. Embrace the transformation that has taken place in your life, it is just noticeable and for those that don't see it, they don't want to see it, but you are definitely not a waste. I'm excited to see where God takes you from here because I know the outcome is going to be great. Always know that I am rooting for you and that I love you, but most importantly remember, you are a Beautiful Wait.

DEATH AND LIFE

People are quick to speak a death sentence over someone's life. Death and life is in the power of your tongue, and they that love it shall eat the fruit thereof. Proverbs 18:21 KJV Holy Bible.

What you speak out of your mouth reflects who you are as a person. If you speak blessings, your life will reflect the life of blessings. If you speak words of cursing's, damnation, negativity, and sickness, your life will depict the negative verbiage you speak out of your mouth. Word curses are just as real as blessings.

Think for a moment back when you were a child on the playground. Remember how those little stick-a-bugs would get stuck to your pant legs? When you looked down at your pant leg, you saw five to ten stick-a-bugs, but when you lifted up your pant leg, you had another ten to twenty stick-a-bugs stuck to your socks which hurt when they touched your skin.

Those stick-a-bugs represent the negative word curses that have been or are currently being spoken over your life. They hurt, stick and poke you like negative words. Just when you thought you'd gotten them all off your pant leg or socks, there was another one hidden that you had forgotten about or didn't know was there.

It is imperative to be conscience of the things we allow people to speak over our lives. It is vital to always speak life even when the situation looks bleak. Death and life is in the power of your tongue. What words are you speaking out of your mouth?

Did you know that research studies shows it takes ten positive words to offset one negative word? Let that sink in for a moment. 10 to 1. That means it takes one negative word to diminish the ten positive words that were spoken over your life, that's why it's important to believe and know what God says about you.

It is amazing to me that man can tame the tongue of a wild beast but, the smallest member in the body of a human (the tongue) cannot be tamed. The tongue has the power to make or break lives, ruin relationships and destroy churches.

Like my grandmother once said, "Don't let your mouth write a check that your behind can't cash." In other words, watch your mouth; because once words are spoken, you can't take them back.

NAVIGATING THROUGH WORDS

Thinking about the conversation that I had with my cousin, I was still somewhat confounded in my mind, "Was I a waste?" Clearly at this this age in my life I shouldn't be trying to figure out my worth of who or what I was. My mind was like a maze all over the place, going in many directions. Here I was navigating through words, repeatedly reminding myself of who God said I was. I'm the apple of his eye, I'm above and not beneath, I am the head and not the tail, etc., but I was still unsure and neither was I convinced.

GIRL GET YOUR FIGHT BACK

When the idea of A Next Level Shift, Volume III, "Girl Get Your Fight Back," was mentioned and the title was introduced, I was thinking to myself, I don't know how to fight. I have never had to fight, not to mention I did not know how to defend myself. I never had to do any of those things, my younger sister always defended or fought for me.

Clearly I couldn't go outside kicking, punching and swinging my arms vigorously knowing I had no opponent to fight with that I could physically see. The battle was in my mind. The battle I was fighting was not a visible confrontation, it was a mental fight. I was in a mind battle fighting with the words of another individual that left me feeling worthless. I told myself, "Tina it's now time you learn to fight, this fight isn't physical. This fight is mental as well as spiritual. No one can fight this fight for you, you've got to fight this battle alone, you and God." For the weapons of our warfare are not carnal, but mighty through God, to the pulling down of strongholds. 2 Corinthians 10:4 KJV.

Put on your spiritual boxing gloves; get in the ring and fight. FIGHT TINA! You are not a waste, but you are a Beautiful Wait. GIRL FIGHT! Fight with the word of God. Put on the whole armor of

God, that ye may be able to stand against the wiles (tricks, schemes, ploys, word curses) of the devil , Ephesians 6:11 KJV. YOU ARE NOT A WASTE! You are a Beautiful Wait . You are loved; you are more than enough; you are deserving; you are the apple of God's eye; you are GOOD; you are not your past; you will not fail; you will not lose. You are more than a conquer; YOU'RE A WINNER!

FLOAT LIKE A BUTTERFLY STING LIKE A BEE

Duck, dodge, punch and weave through the blows of the enemy by fasting, praying, worshipping, and praising. In the words of the late, great heavyweight boxer Muhammad Ali, "Float like a butterfly, sting like a bee," keep fighting don't quit. When the devil tells you what you're not, remind him of who you are. When he dares to remind you of your past, remind him of his future, "In hell will you lift up your eyes". When the enemy says, "you're a waste" punch him with a right jab, and let him know that everything God created he said, "and it was good."

When he says, "you're a failure," punch him with a quick right jab to the torso and tell him that,"you're more than a conqueror." When the enemy punches you in the stomach, "and tells youthat you are not loved," hit him with a one-two drill, then with an uppercut and tell him that,

"No greater love than this than a man lay down his life for a friend." No matter what combination of negative blows the devil comes up with, keep fighting.

Hear me when I say, that God is an identity changer and no matter what your past has been, you are no longer identified by your use-to-be's. God has thrown your yesterday's into the sea of forgetfulness to remember them no more. Maybe your past was ugly, and as hard as it is to believe, someone just might see you as a waste, but there are more people for you, that are against you. There's someone who sees you as a beautiful wait . They see you as a diamond in the rough and they're waiting for you to be polished and sharpened. Genuinely, there are people cheering and waiting for you to blossom into that beautiful swan that you are becoming.

Please don't quit fighting. Although, you may never know it, God has his prayer warriors, praying and interceding on your behalf. When you get a little winded while in the fight, he has his intercessors right there to wipe the sweat from your brow and to give you a drink. They are there cheering you on to fight.

God came that we might have life and life more abundantly. He wants us to win in every aspect of our lives. He has great expectations for us, his children, and it is his desire that we stay in the ring and fight. Just like Jesus was in the fiery furnace with the three Hebrew boys (Daniel Chapter 3), he's also in the ring of life with us today.

The devil is on his job daily as an identity thief. In John 10:10 the Bibles states, "The thief comes only to steal, kill and destroy..." The devil is taking his job seriously and he knows that his time is swiftly coming to an end, so he has to constantly devise a plan to knock us off kilter and to keep throwing blows.

Psalm 144:1 states, "Blessed be the Lord my strength which teaches my hands to war and my fingers to fight..." With God as our trainer, we can't lose. We can't lose because God has showed us how to fight the enemy with his word. People of God; God is our shield and buckler, he's in the fight with us, which means the fight is fixed... WE WIN.

Girl, put on your boxing gloves and get in the ring. If you're like me and you've never had a fight, fight anyway. If you're afraid, fight anyway. Remember God has not given you the spirit of fear but of power, love and a sound mind. If this fight is one of many that you may have lost, go into the ring believing that you've already won. Either way, get in the ring and fight because your life literally depends on it. The battle is not yours, it's the Lords, remember...

You're a Beautiful Wait. YOU WIN!

Now get in the ring and fight with all your might. Remember the fight is fixed and you WIN!

God is in the ring with you and the angel in heaven are cheering for you. You are literally in the fight of your life. Don't look to the right, nor to the left. FIGHT! Girl get your fight back.

Casonya Carter

MY GENESIS
"I'M LIVING A NEW LIFE"

Excerpts from prophecy given to me in 2012-2013 by two well-known Bishops:

"The Holy Ghost told me to tell you that He has not forgotten the promises He gave you over 35 years ago. The word of God says, He is getting ready to make the promises of your past to be the present of your now."

"Once you see yourself for who you really are from your Genesis, then God will make you stronger and allow who is for you to see the true you. The Holy Ghost wants me to inform you that, 'I did all that pulmonary talk for you cause you are going to be helping women everywhere you go. I just set precedent for you to regurgitate it in your own style.' The Lord says, 'Begin to write tidbits of things you hear me say and others say. Put them in a book.' The Lord says, Look for the great things in life beginning February 5, 2013.' Just strive for all you need in Him."

WHEN YOU CAN HEAL, YOU CAN REVEAL

I was having one of those moments when I am my own worst critic; feeling that I should be further along than I am in life. So I do what deescalates my stress; I go window-shopping and sometimes, I just shop. I was in Burlington's and saw this inspirational frame which read, "If you don't believe in miracles, perhaps you have forgotten you are one." God used that frame to change my whole perspective that day. While lying in bed that evening, the quote, "When you can heal, you can reveal" was birthed and integrated into my spirit when life for me, was coming full circle. I was reflecting on my life and looking at what God had done to get me through some of the worst, yet best times of my life. When I see God in the midst of it all, I can use the words "worst" and "best" in the same sentence because it helped shape me into the woman of God I am today. I have been taught, that for every storm, there is a purpose. Even when I am obedient to God, storms will still come. That was the toughest concept for me to accept. It helped me, however, to understand that in the darkest part of our storm that is where our blessings will be found.

Frustrated, I did not know what to do. Here I was all alone; a silent hot mess. I thought about a late night text, "Tough Season, Tougher GOD" that I received from my First Lady. I was recuperating at home from an episode of my Ulcerative Colitis/Crohns. Remembering God is bigger than anything I may be facing, I just needed to rely on my faith; Faith that can conquer anything.

God birthed in my spirit the Seven D's of my life; Disease, Death, Divorce, Depression, Deliverance, Discovery and Destiny; to get to what I call "My Genesis: A New Chapter In My Life." This realization gave me a whole new insight to 2 Corinthians 5:17, "Therefore if any man be in Christ, he is a new creature: old things are passed away; behold, all things are become new" (The King James Version-KJV).

DISEASE

In the summer of 2005, after dealing with months of health challenges, I had just come home from a week-long stay in the hospital. My stomach was in knots; I was cramping really badly. I did not have a major appetite. I was very weak; something was not right. I was staying with my dad because my husband was working the night shift. Yes, I am a daddy's girl. The next day, I could not keep food down. Then the ultimate fear, I was bleeding every time I went to the bathroom. I was so weak that I crawled up the stairs and my dad had to rush me to the hospital.

I was in severe pain.

The last thing I remember was getting pain medicine and the worried look on my father and sister-in-law's face. I woke up with faces looking down on me. I recall the doctor saying, "Welcome back kiddo; we almost lost you. Had you waited one more day, we would not be having this conversation." I learned that the doctors performed emergency surgery when they discovered a bowel obstruction and blood clots throughout my body. The bowel obstructions resulted in having about 15 inches of my intestines removed, being placed in a medically induced coma and I suffered a stroke that caused my left side to be paralyzed. Tears began to flow- I was only 41. My entire left side was paralyzed; I didn't want to believe it. All the activity of my limbs were dead and I was very weak. I had a feeding tube and was hooked up to all types of devices: pick lines in both arms, oxygen tube and other monitoring devices.

The doctors were uncertain if the paralysis would be temporary, only time would tell. The fear of hearing this devastated me. I was so shaken by the mere thought that I may never walk again. I looked towards Heaven and started praying to God. I was scared but I knew that God had me. In the early hours of the morning, I would cry out to God. Tears would roll down my face; I could not wipe them. My family, friends, my church, my students, colleagues, my neighbors and my community were all praying. A nurse said she thought that I was famous because there were so many people in the waiting room praying for me.

Even in the midst of it all, I never lost my hope or faith. Then it happened; I sneezed the feeding tube out. When the nurse and doctors came in, they opted out of putting the tube back in, tested the feeling in my legs and they moved. I began working with the physical and occupational therapist. I thought because my legs were moving and I was sitting up, I would be walking out the door to my home. However, when they stood me up, my legs gave out on me. Fighting back tears, I asked them to give me some time to myself; I just needed some alone time with God. I travailed all that night. The next day I went forth in Jesus' name.

I spent the whole summer of 2005 in the hospital. I was moved to Mary Free Bed Rehabilitation Center. The road to recovery has not always been easy. I've encountered several flare-ups over the years that required working with my Gastrologist at the University of Michigan. I call Crohns and Ulcerative Colitis the silent disease; you can look great on the outside but your insides can be in great turmoil. I am continuing to learn how to manage this disease. I have a great support system with the Crohns and Colitis Foundation and others who battle chronic diseases. I refuse to let this condition beat me; I will beat it. With God, I have gone from a four prong cane to running my first 10k in spring of 2017 and my second in May of 2017.

DEATH

Why me Lord? Why did I have to lose my mom in a tragic car accident at the age of eight? Why did I have to lose both set of grandparents? As much as I love kids, why did I have to experience a miscarriage? In 2010, my marriage died, I lost my dad, my first lady and my mentor to cancer—all in the matter of 6 months. In addition, I still struggle from the side effects from my near death experience. "LORD! Do you hear me?" I cried in my home alone, "WHY ME?" Broken and dying a slow death inside, I could hear a small voice in my spirit saying "Why not me?" This was bigger than me. The pain inside was starting to heal me from the inside out.

DIVORCE

"You don't look like you are going through a divorce." That is what I would hear from time to time. Someone please tell me, what does divorce look like? I never thought it would happen to me, especially since I waited until I was in my late 30's to get married. So much was happening in the marriage. I was dealing with how to be a wife with an illness in my life. My husband was dealing with the loss of a job. Neither of us knew how to deal with these major life changes.

I turned to being busy at work and singing and directing the choir to prove that I was back to my "old" self. My husband turned to things that clouded his judgement which led to various forms of infidelity. I could not believe that we allowed the enemy to side track us. After the divorce was final, I went through counseling. My prayer was "Lord make me better, not bitter."

I asked the Lord to show "me" and heal me from the inside out. I did not want to continue to focus on the past seasons of my life, I wanted to be the woman He called me to be in this season of my life. This allowed me to heal and forgive. I had a talk with my ex and told him what God was calling me to do. He told me that he recognized the call on my life and to follow through on what God called me to do. What I was not going to do whenever I spoke/wrote about the demise of the marriage was bash him.

I want to empower people so that they will not allow the enemy to hold them hostage because their marriage did not work. I learned the importance of allowing God in every area of the marriage; as a couple, in your individual endeavors and struggles, your triumphs and your setbacks. You can't just pick and choose when you want God to handle things. It is all or nothing. Therefore, just like in all things we must give thanks, in all things we must have Christ.

I remember my Bishop, William C. Abney, saying, "In marriage the farther you are from Christ, the farther you are from each other. This is so true. When you allow too much space, you allow too much room for the enemy to interfere in the marriage. Remember John 10:10 (The King James Version-KJV) tells us that the enemy comes to kill, steal and destroy; God comes that we may have life, and have it to the fullest. Marriage is a covenant relationship that must be protected by God at all times.

DEPRESSION

Just faking it 'till I make it. I was hurting really badly. Every area of my life was in disarray: personal, professional and physical. Personally my family of origin was gone; No parents, no grandparents on either side. I was single, no kids and not dating. Professionally I was experiencing one of the worst times in my career. I encountered my first experience of microaggressions and bullies in the workplace. My Crohns/UC was taking its toll on my body. The medicines were causing weight gain and other unpleasant side effects. In public I was still strong, supportive, the one that people came to for encouragement and uplifting. I did not know how to truly help myself. In private, I was a "hot mess". I slept on the couch 80% of the time and I would stay extremely busy so I had no time to think about my life; at least I thought. I did just enough to stay afloat. I was at the lowest of lows in my life.

I hosted Thanksgiving at my home and we had a great time. However, my family noticed that I was not my normal, bubbly self. What I was dealing with on the inside was surfacing on the outside. I was allowing the enemy to take me into that dark place. I was functioning but I was depressed. I was feeling like Job and so I took on his mentality "Thou He slay me, yet will I trust HIM."

After Thanksgiving, I knew I had to take my faith in God to another dimension. Waiting until Sunday was not an option, I needed God right now. My living room became a sanctuary. On my knees I cried out to the Lord; I needed Him like I never needed Him before. I sought Christian Counseling from a faith based practice with a counselor who was a believer. God blessed me with two great support groups: Sisters Taking Action to Reverse Statistics (S.T.A.R.S.) and Soulful Motion. The foundation of these groups are faith based to strengthen your mind, body and soul through sharing, empowering, and uplifting each other in prayer that included a health/workout component. Daily we came together to pray, share what God has done or is doing in our lives, and then we workout.

DELIVERANCE

I had suppressed some insecurities and kept them hidden deep for so long. I struggled with being dark-skinned, never feeling that I was light or white enough for a position or a relationship as well as trying to debunk the myths that society has about dark-skinned woman. I've always been a "thick chick." But inwardly, I never embraced it. What I was experiencing personally and professionally allowed those insecurities to resurface and affected my self-esteem. I had to face my demons that had been holding me captive.

Listening to the song by Kurt Carr "For Every Mountain" got me through many hard days. God delivered me from people. Personally and professionally, I could no longer allow people to detour me from where God has me in this season of my life. His purpose for my life is not about them; it is about HIM. I've learned how to love the skin in. I'm a dark-skinned daughter of the King. I'm smart and intelligent. I'm curvy, fearfully and wonderfully made by God. I'm unique; the only "me" there is. No one can be/do what He designed me to be/do. I am still here and it's by the Grace of God. I took some time to examine, reflect, and be real honest with myself. I had to learn how to spend meaningful time with God. I learned how to truly love ME.

I had to set standards, not boundaries, in every area of my life. Especially with the individuals that I allowed to get close to me in the area of dating. No more a Princess looking for Prince charming to sweep her off her feet. I had a Queen's mentality, fully believing there is a King that He is preparing just for me for this latter season of my life.

DISCOVERY

I discovered who Cassonya really is. God started moving me out of my comfort zone. I realize more than ever that He had to get me alone to minister to me so that I could hear from Him. This has allowed Him to heal in every area that I hurt. It was a lonely and scary place. Once I started to embrace what God was doing in my life, my desire to know God more increased and my relationship with Him became stronger. I won't compromise it for anything in this world. I just want to be the woman of God that stands on His word and shares what He has done in the midst of it all.

DESTINY

I understand my assignment now much clearer than ever before. It was a set up. My life has a whole new meaning. I was thinking I needed to be some scripture quoting person to witness. God pointed me in the direction that people need to feel His love through the words He gives me to encourage them and speak life to their situation. Therefore, if I am ministering through song and/or words, I realize that my ministry is to share who God is and how He can redirect/change lives.

I always knew my calling in life was to touch people's lives, make a difference and give back as a mentor/encourager. Knowing God's will for my life, I know what my purpose in Him is all about. The Seven D's of my life have helped me solidify my purpose to be that difference, even when it's not popular. My purpose is bigger than I, myself. It's not about me anymore.

Whatever I do, I will represent Christ at all times. I want to make God happy with me. Even in my worst day, He still makes me HAPPY. And for this I give God PRAISE!

"For Every Mountain"

By Kurt Carr

I've got so much to thank God for
So many wonderful blessings and so many open doors
A brand new mercy
Along with each new day
That's why I praise You
And for this I give You praise
For waking me up this morning
For starting me on my way
For letting me see the sunshine of a brand new day
A brand new mercy along with each new day
You're Jehovah Jireh
You've been my provider
So many times You rescued me, so many times You supplied my need

I want to thank You for the blessings You give to me each day
For every mountain You brought me over
For every trial you've seen me through
For every blessing, Hallelujah, for this I give You praise

References:

- Kurt Carr (1997) For Every Mountain. [Recorded by Kurt Carr], on Kurt Carr Singers
– No One Else, [Gospel] Recoded live in Los Angeles. GospoCentric, Inc. Cite

Shawanda Tumblin

I HAVE SINNED NOW WHERE DO I GO FROM HERE? LORD, I'M NOT WORTHY OF YOUR GRACE

Born to seventeen year old parents with absolutely no clue as to how to raise a child, my father's parents stepped in to help. If I had ten thousand tongues, I couldn't possibly thank God enough for allowing this to happen. I was the apple of their eye, their first grandchild, they loved me like I was a precious gift from God and were very proud of me. You see, they were faith filled people who loved God with all their hearts and they wanted to make sure that I had a relationship with HIM as well. As I write this, I can still hear my grandmother's sweet southern voice calling me and my aunt's name every Sunday morning to make sure we were up and ready in time for Sunday School. I actively served in many different ministries and because of my involvement in the church, I was well known and liked by many, especially adults; some even called me a role model. The church was proud of me and so was my grandparents. I was "the good girl". Life was great. Now that you have an idea of my background you will understand how I hurt/disappointed so many people.

In the summer of my fifteenth birthday I started my first part-time job at a youth center. This is where I met HIM. He was nice, funny, intriguing and though I didn't know it at the time, ten years older than myself. Each day he would walk pass my window smiling so of course I started smiling back; this led to him stopping into the office to converse and make me laugh. At age 15, I was nerdy, really thin, awkward looking, but mature and dressed professionally, oh and definitely interested in dating as most girls are at this age. My boss noticed the flirtation and kindly warned me to stay away from him as he was too old for me, but by this time I was already intrigued. I mean how much older could he be? I would soon find out… We had great conversations and laughed a lot, "he surely couldn't be more than a few years older," I thought. The summer ended and so did my job assignment. We exchanged phone numbers to keep in touch and a few months went past and we hadn't contacted each other. Then, one day I received a letter in the mail and it was from him. More followed. As he was much older and more experienced he knew how to peek my interests. When I turned 16, we started dating and my family absolutely loved him and his family loved me as well. I found out not long after that he was 26. He told me by giving me his driver's license and telling me to look at his date of birth. My boss was correct and now I knew why he'd given me the warning.

After finding out his age, I tried to keep the relationship from my church family because I didn't want them to know that I wasn't as good of a girl as they thought, but as the saying goes, "what's done in the dark always comes to light." As our relationship grew, church members, whom I admired, began to talk to me about him and let me know how he wasn't right for me; but all of their words went in one ear and out the other. I thought I was mature enough to be in this relationship and soon started skipping church.

"I think I'll wear this dress today," I thought as I looked in my closet. "Maybe no one will notice my pudge." I already broke the news to my family and now how would I face my church members? This was harder for me because I knew I wouldn't be able to serve in the ministries and everyone would know why. It wasn't long before everyone knew and I started to see staring and disgust on some of their faces. One person had no problem telling me how disappointed they were in me and how they'd thought I would actually do something great with my life and never thought I'd wind up as another statistic. This really hit me hard as more people that I admired said similar things to me, so eventually I stopped attending church altogether. I guess they were right, I was an unwed child having a child. The shame set in. Would I be a statistic? I was a senior in high school, would I even graduate?

GRADUATION & MOTHERHOOD

Today I graduate from high school, yes I made it! Through it all, I made it! They said I wouldn't finish high school because I got pregnant, but I proved them wrong and I did it! Though I'd achieved this goal, there was no open house for me and no celebrations.

Three months later, my life changed forever. I would no longer just be a teenager, today another title would be added to my resume'... ***MOTHER***. Wow, where do I go from here? I'm unmarried, being talked about and told I will never amount to anything because I had a baby out of wedlock. I feel like a disgrace to my family and church because I've sinned and the side looks, hurtful remarks and stares seem to seep into my soul. No one loves me anymore. I've completely let everyone down. Again, I thought,

Maybe they are right.

Maybe I won't amount to anything.

Maybe my life *IS* over.....

I can't go to college now nor can I leave my child with my mom as she has 6 more children to raise and besides he is my responsibility; so I guess this is it for me. I'm only a kid myself really but now I have to be an adult. I am seriously second guessing my relationship and my future at this point. I don't know what to do.

WHAT IF I PRAYED, WOULD GOD HEAR ME?

Wait a minute, I've been taught my whole life that prayer is the key and faith unlocks the door but at this point if church members are disappointed in me, I'm sure Jesus is not trying to hear my prayers. I'm going to give it a try anyway and see what happens. I began to see things a little differently now.

I decided to enroll at the local business college to ensure a better future for myself and my child. I knew it would be hard but I believed God would help me through it. After the first year I felt like it was time for me to move out of my mom's house into my own apartment with my one year old son. Attending classes during the day, taking care of a baby, working part-time at the college and doing homework at night while trying to maintain a relationship with my son's father almost caused me to have a nervous breakdown. One day I walked into my apartment and just started crying uncontrollably and couldn't stop. Once the tears stopped flowing I realized that I was literally juggling all of this by myself and this relationship wasn't going anywhere and it wasn't what I envisioned for my life. So at age 19, three years after it all started, I ended it. I began to realize that I wanted more in my life and God had made me stronger than I'd ever thought and given me the strength to carry the load that I held.

I continued in college and began dating again, but just didn't seem to find what I was looking for in a guy. Negative thoughts began to enter my mind," Who was going to want a single mother?" I prayed with tears streaming.. "Lord, please send the man that you have for me and let him know me when he sees me and let me know him when I see him."

At age 20, I met my HIM, the man that would become the love of my life. He was everything that I'd prayed for and then some. When I first laid eyes on him, he took my breath away. I asked a friend who he was and his response was "He is the perfect guy for you, corny jokes and all". This friend was not one to lie to me so I asked him to introduce me but I wasn't aware of the unconventional way he was going to do so. My future husband was walking toward me and my friend waited for the perfect time and pushed us into each other. I looked up into his big brown beautiful eyes and said, "hi," and my future husband replied, "Is that all you wanted to say?" We both laughed and the conversation sparked that night has lasted more than 23 years. He was 3 years older than I and home from college. I was still in college.

When I told him that I had a two year old son, I thought it would scare him off, but it didn't. The first test was meeting my son to see how they interacted and they loved each other from the start. The second test was introducing him to my family and they loved him as well. He was genuine, a gentleman, kind-hearted, intelligent, Christian, encouraged me daily and oh so handsome. After about 10 months, he asked me to marry him. We were engaged for a little over a year and at age 22, I graduated college. Two months later we were married and will celebrate 22 years of marriage in 2018.

We have raised 3 children together and are truly best friends. People around me predicted my future, but they were wrong. You see, they were looking through the eyes of their flesh and couldn't possibly see or even fathom how God was going to use someone like me who had made mistakes. Looking back on this part of my life, I can truly say, "what he had planned for me was better than anything I could've imagined for myself. He is the author of my life and my journey is not over, my next chapter is starting." He's not done writing your story either. I've listed a few steps below that I wish I'd known back then to help me in my time of need. I know them now, so I am sharing them with you. The one step I was aware of was step #1 which was the most important, the others came in time.

STEPS TO GETTING YOUR FIGHT BACK!

If you or someone you know is in a situation like this:

Step #1(**PRAYER**)-Recognize it is the trick of the enemy to discourage you from prayer because prayer changes things. You are NOT alone! God **IS** listening to your prayers. **Prayer doesn't cost you anything, but through prayer, you gain everything!**" *Call unto me, and I will answer thee, and show thee great and mighty things, which thou knowest not." Jeremiah 33:3 KJV*

Step #2-(**GOD's GUIDANCE**)- Ask God for guidance for your life. Being a parent can be hard, especially as a teenager, but if you ask God for guidance for your future, he will direct your steps. **For me, He blessed me to finish college , get married, find a good job, raise my family, etc. and for you it could be totally different but whatever HIS plan is, He knows what is best for you, believe me.** *"If any of you lack wisdom, let him ask God, that giveth to all men liberally, and upbraideth not; and it shall be given him. But let him ask in faith, nothing wavering. For he that wavereth is like a wave of the sea driven with the wind and tossed. For let not that man think that he shall receive anything of the LORD. A double minded man is unstable in all his ways. James 1:5-8 KJV*

Step #3-(**STUDY**)- Get your hands on a bible or bible app and begin to read and study it so that you have the strength to press on when you feel like giving up. When you study the word and begin to understand it, the enemy has to come up with new strategies to attack you. **The bible is everywhere now so you have access to it at all times.** *"Study to shew thyself approved unto God, a workman that needeth not to be ashamed, rightly dividing the word of truth" 2 Timothy 2:15, KJV*

Step #4- (**PROMISES**)- Search the scriptures for God's promises over your life and begin to speak them over yourself and your child/children. God has many promises and once you realize that he is not a man that he should lie, what he says, he does, then you will begin to recognize those promises being fulfilled in your own life. **God continues to give us another chance, once you repent from your heart, he throws that into the sea of forgetfulness and you get a "Do Over". So your old self is your past. Let it stay there and walk in his truth from that day forward.** One of my favorite scriptures is *"Therefore if any man be in Christ, he is a new creature: old things are passed away; behold, all things are become new."2 Corinthians 5:17 KJV*

Step #5-**(PUT ON YOUR ARMOUR)**- I like to say " get suited up!" Once the enemy sees that you don't believe his lies and you are getting stronger in the Lord, he is going to try to hit you wherever he can to discourage you and make you feel depressed, defeated and worthless but that's when you pull out the Word of God, that you've been studying for times such as these and believe me sis, there will be times. *Put on the whole armour of God, that ye may be able to stand against the wiles of the devil." Ephesians 6:11 KJV*

Step #6-**(GOD'S REPORT vs. MAN's REPORT)** This last step is to remind you that even when the world looks down upon you, points fingers at you and speaks negativity over your life; God still loves you! He can still use you! HE has a plan for your life! He says:

You are fearfully and wonderfully made….Psalm 139:14

He has made you in HIS image and given you dominion over every creeping thing upon the earth..Genesis 1:26

Most importantly, you are a child of God… 1 John 3:2

Who hath believed our report? And to whom is the arm of the Lord revealed? Isaiah 53:1KJV

So whose report will you believe about yourself? God's or Man's? I choose to believe God's report because he created us and I hope you do too.

Once you have learned and applied these steps to your life, you are on your way to getting your fight back!

Anna L. Crockett

GIRL GET YOUR FIGHT BACK PIECE BY PIECE

"And the rest, some on boards, and some on broken pieces of the ship. And so it came to pass, that they escaped all safe to land." Act 27: 1-44. This particular passage of scripture describes how Paul and other prisoners were on a ship to Italy to be imprisoned but because of a tumultuous storm the ship was destroyed. But Paul, the prisoners and crewmen landed safely on dry land sailing on broken pieces of the ship.

In life, we sometimes are forced to sail through life on broken pieces until we gain the strength to abandon the pieces and *Fight Back*!

My journey of living life on broken pieces began on Sunday, June 30, 1991 at 5:30a.m. My life was shattered; I was tossed two and fro like the ship mentioned in the Book of Acts. I received a phone call from one of the mothers of our church. Her voice was hysterical and panicky, she said, "Anna, Come Quickly," my neighbor was taking his morning walk and your daughter is lying on her front side walk in a pool of blood. Those words were gut wrenching, I tried to comprehend what I thought I heard, my heart skipped beats and it seemed as if it took forever to get to her house which was only about 15 blocks away.

When my younger daughter, granddaughter and I arrived, there were fire trucks, police cars and people everywhere. My daughter, my first born was lying lifeless with a white sheet covering her. My daughter and I lost it, I remember my daughter and a friend of our family swiftly taking my 5 ½ year old granddaughter away; this was her mother lying there covered with a sheet.

After what seemed like hours, I could only think; How could this be? What happened? Who would hurt my daughter? And why? We had talked the night before and planned to see each other at church the next morning, this had to be a nightmare and I was praying that I would soon wake up, but I never woke up! Even at times now, it seems like a bad dream.

My 34-year-old sister and my mother passed away 3 months of each other; although my mother was ill, but as I think back, I can relate to why she died so soon after my sister's death, her heart had been broken into pieces. She had lost her baby and it was unbearable for her. I hurt when I lost my mother and my sister but to lose a child is an unimaginable hurt that no one can explain unless they have gone through it themselves. A mother carries an invisible umbilical cord of her children; thus, she carries them when they hurt and when they are happy but when one of them dies a mother's entire inside is crushed into pieces.

As days passed, I literally walked on broken pieces because my heart was broken, and my entire body hurt all over. I went through the motions of taking care of her 2 children, making funeral arrangements and enduring my last goodbyes to my sweet daughter and facing the reality that she was gone and not coming back.

After weeks of turmoil; talking to detectives, the local newspaper, family and friends, I felt as if I couldn't go on, this burden was much too much to bear. My heart was broken, and I didn't know when it would ever be fixed or if it could be.

I thank God for my family, friends and church family, when I couldn't pray for myself I felt surrounded by love and prayers. They meant well, and I appreciated their prayers, their offers of sympathy, empathy and willing to do whatever they could. It's difficult to explain but when you are hurting, you hear individuals talking to you, but you don't hear a word of what they are saying, it seems as their words were falling on deaf ears.

I was in the valley of sorrow and despair. I wanted my daughter back and I wanted answers, why would an all loving God allow this to happen to my child. It was too hard to comprehend. It was only the word of God that gives you comfort when you are in a valley of sorrow and hurt. Even then, it was God's word that gave me strength to keep going. I quoted I Thessalonians 5;18 '*In everything give thanks: for this is the will of God in Christ Jesus concerning you*(me). I walked and prayed constantly I was not thanking God for what happened to my daughter, but I was thanking Him because of his greatness, his goodness and his mercy; although my heart was shattered into pieces, I trusted Him.

After my daughter's death, there were so many speculations regarding her death; drugs, lovers quarrel, and revenge but none of that mattered, whatever the reason she was murdered, it was not going to bring her back, she was gone forever!

For years, I didn't trust anyone, especially her so called friends. Everyone I saw, I thought could this be the person that had murdered my daughter. After all, it was speculated by the detectives that she knew the perpetrators and she had opened the door for them, this was the reason why she was on the side walk.

My daughter was beautiful both inside and out. She was a home bodied type of person and never bother anyone, she was very trusting and took people at face value. She did not smoke, drink or do drugs. She loved the Lord; her family and she had a special love for her children. She had been stabbed 26 times, who would do such a thing and why? To this day, her murder is unsolved and is in the cold case file. Every anniversary of her death, a cold case detective stops in to visit me to give me assurance that she is not forgotten. One detective in particular would often tell me that he was going to stay on the case even after retirement because he knew the killer is out there and she or he (they) will manifest themselves in some way or another sooner or later.

Several cold cases have been solved due to modern technology and I'm believing if God does it for others, he is going to do the same thing for our family. We realize that finding her killer(s) will not bring her back, but it will bring closure to our family and we will rest in knowing that her death has been vindicated.

Even as I write, I feel the same gut wrenching feeling as I did on that Sunday morning, June 30, 1991. **Getting Your Fight Back** is not an easy thing to do. Sometimes it was a fight just to get out of bed. All my children were adults and now I had to raise a 5 ½ year-old granddaughter and a 3, year old grandson, but every day I count it a blessing and I thank God and their biological father for giving me the opportunity to raise my grandchildren. Although they were young, they had suffered a great loss and they were going through a great adjustment. To wake up and find out that they would never to see their mother again, never to see her laughter, her sweet smile or a simple hug was overwhelming. Those were just a few of **NEVERS** that they would experience in life without their mother; high school and college graduations, proms, weddings, and grandchildren. I was in pain, but they were also.

As a side note, when tragedy happens or things that you have no control over and you cannot seem to handle, even with God; it's alright to seek professional help; this is what their father and I did for my grandchildren. My faith has been and always will be in God, but they needed something different. we choose to seek professional help for them. I realized that I would never take the place of their mother, but I would give them all the love, encouragement and support that is within me.

My heart was broken, and I had to consider not only my grandchildren but my children also, they had lost a big sister, the one they loved, looked up to, fought with and had fun with. At family gatherings her siblings still joke about the things she said and did when they were growing up.

Getting my Fight Back was not easy. This was exceptionally hard for me because my place of worship and employment is directly across the street where she lived and died. For months, I could not allow myself to pass her house to go to work or church, I had to take an alternate route just to get there. It was an hour by hour, day by day process with a lot of praying.

God knew before she was conceived that at age 28, on June 30, 1991 her life would be taken from her. God is not a God of darkness but a God of light, He didn't cause my daughter's death, He also knows that the prince of the air is lurking, seeking whom he can destroy, and He allowed the enemy to take my daughter's life. God allows dreadful things to happen to good people. She was a good daughter, yet God allowed this to happen to her, He had the power to prevent it, but he choose not to!

Getting your Fight Back requires making a special effort to push forward but most of all, it's imperative to trust God and relying totally on Him to put the pieces back together. It's normal to mourn and there is no time table because each person is different, but we shouldn't moan nor wallow in our sorrow. A loss is devastating but we cannot allow it to define who we are or take ones' identity

Getting your Fight Back requires doing something that you never did before! I never liked gardening, but we had an abundance of flowers, so I planted them in her memory. This helped me to relax and to take pride in the ultimate results. To this day, I plant flowers each year. I also, went to school for to become a Balloon Decorator and started a business in her honor **"Balloons for Frieda."**.

Getting your Fight Back requires fighting for your sanity, because there are times when you feel that you are losing your mind. *Fight the Good Fight of Faith*!

Getting your Fight Back requires Remembering her smile, the way she walked and talked. Remembering the times, we shared together, whether in agreement with each other or agreeing to disagree. And most of all remembering that Life Goes On!

Getting your Fight Back requires confessing to God that you are angry, hurt and disappointed and you can't understand why He would allow this to happen to your child.

Getting your Fight Back requires seeing her in her children. Seeing her features in them, the same gestures that she made, or enjoying the same foods that their mother enjoyed.

We can make it on broken pieces and evidently the pieces will come together, and you will get your **Fight Back** in unimaginable ways. After all, we have God on our side. My favorite scriptures are; Psalms 124:1(a) **"If it had not been for the Lord who was on our (Anna's) side, where would I be."** Philippians 4:13 *"I can do all thing through Christ which strengthens me."* I believe what I read, and I believe that whatever concerns me concerns Him. We serve a compassionate Father who is always with us and will never forsake us.

Getting your Fight Back requires Healing, Allow God to heal your hurt. Only God can take the pain away but its in His timing. Everyone hurts in diverse ways; thus, everyone heals differently but we must allow the healing process to take place. *"**He heals the broken-hearted and bandages their wounds**. Psalm 147:3

Getting your Fight Back requires forgiveness, how can we forgive someone who has taken your child's life and broken the family cords. It may take years to get to this point, but with the help of the Lord, it can be done. It's a must! Unforgiveness blocks our blessings. **"But if ye forgive not men their trespasses, neither will your Father forgive your trespasse**s."

Getting your Fight Back requires Expectancy, Expecting the unexpected. Believing that I will see her again in heaven. Expecting that the person who killed her would someday come forward or the individual(s) who knew what happened and would feel remorseful and turn the perpetrator in.

Getting your Fight Back requires being grateful, Grateful for the years that you shared together, grateful that her children didn't get hurt on that dreadful morning, and that she left a part of herself with us to care for.

Getting your Fight Back requires sharing with others who have lost children, giving them love, support and the assurance that God loves them, and He will bring them through. My dear friend lost 3 children; one at 3 months old, another at 6 years old and her only son at age 30. After my daughter was killed, she would pick me up and take me for long rides without saying anything. Other times, she would talk about the loss of her children; (this was before her son had passed away). I could feel her hurt but I knew that if God had brought her through, He would do the same for me if I opened my heart and allowed him.

Getting your Fight Back requires trusting God to give you strength for each day. "***Trust in the Lord with all thine heart, lean not to thine own understandin***g, Proverbs 5:3.

Getting your Fight Back after losing a child or a loved one does not mean that you have forgotten them, nor does it mean that you won't hurt anymore. What it does mean is that you love them, you miss them, and they will never be forgotten because they are tucked away safely in your heart.

> *For I know the thoughts that I think toward you,*
> *saith the Lord, thoughts of peace,*
> *and not of evil, to give you an expected end.*
> Jeremiah 29:11

Carolyn O'Bryant

I AM A SURVIVOR NOT A VICTIM

I awaken out of a deep sleep suddenly thinking that I heard something in the house but everyone was really quiet. I retrieved my phone from the nightstand to check what time it was, it was 3:00AM. I got extremely agitated to the point where it seemed that I couldn't stand being in my own skin anymore. I have never been able to get a full night of sleep since my childhood, but this night was different from any other night when I awakened freaking out.

I couldn't tolerate being in bed any longer, so I jumped up undressed and got into the shower in hopes this would calm my nerves. I just stood under the hot water for approximately ten minutes; although, it seemed like hours. My mind started to focus on my breasts. I just stood there frozen in place saying why, repeatedly to myself. While standing there, I began to touch my right breast to do a self-exam, this is something that I had never done before. I said to myself one more to go girl, but my attitude changed quickly as my body started to shake. My right hand reached for my left breast and I froze, the lump in my breast was as big as my fist. I started to say to myself, no you are making something out of a lump, then my emotions took over and I screamed. Then I lost my balance as I went to my knees, taking the shower curtain with me. Suddenly, everything got so loud and within seconds in my mind, I went straight to death, then to my sons and grandbabies as the tears came rolling down my face uncontrollably.

The next thing I did as I was crying, I started hitting my head against the bathroom shower wall, calling myself stupid and how did I allow this to happen. The sudden knocking on the door shocked me because I thought I was alone a home, but my son was screaming, mom are you okay? I froze from the sound of his voice. Can I come in please? I was sobbing out of control and said No, No, No out loud; what am I going to do? Finally, I got myself under control and I immediately opened the bathroom door and said yes son I am okay; I love you. I will explain to you lather, I promise as I walked pass him to my room hiding my face as I walked. My son followed me right into my room and kept saying, what's wrong, what's wrong mom? He stood there for a moment not believing my reason for being upset. He looked at me saying, mom did someone hurt you? No one has hurt me son, I just found something out and it's upsetting to me a little bit. You go back to bed, I love you.

After he left my room, I immediately ran to my phone to text my girlfriend who lives around the corner from me to tell her what I discovered while doing my breast exam. She tried to calm me down by saying everything will be okay and to make an appointment to see my doctor as soon as possible. Her re-assurance did not help much, my mind was racing, I could not relax or go back to sleep. I laid in bed looking up at the celling; then all of a sudden, my past came back like a movie projector in my head, playing over and over again. I kept hearing these words: I don't love you, you will never matter, you are alone, no one will love you or want you, and you don't exist to me anymore, then dead silence, Mom?

In my mind, I was back home as a child crying wanting to be acknowledged and loved. At age 13, one night I walked out of my house, wondering what did I do? I had nowhere to go except with an abusive man. My eyes jerked opened looking out into the darkness of my room. All I wanted to do is cry and disappear because I was wondering how I was going to fight this battle alone. Then my mind focused back on my mother, I wanted here, why? I guess to tell me everything would be okay. This was very confusing to me because the relationship between my parents and I was dead since I was six years old.

The time was moving slowly as I was sitting up in bed, all I wanted to do was runaway, the pain was great, and it was hurting deep down into my soul. Denial tried to sneak into my thoughts, but I knew in my heart that I had breast cancer. My faith was strong, but I was terrified of the unknown regarding my health and my life. My mind kept going back to my childhood and younger years, a place I promised myself never to revisit. The times that I was homeless, sleeping in abandoned building and on church floors, getting beaten until I passed out or raped repeatedly. The loss of a child that I couldn't grieve for, just to say goodbye and disguise any pain that was visible to the eye. I put my past in a casket to never be opened again because I didn't have time to grieve. I had to raise two boys into amazing men, motherhood took priority for me. I can take care of myself later, after I be the best mom that I can be.

Thus, I removed all people from my life who would remind me of all the destruction in my life and who tried to destroy my peace. Cancer was my enemy now, not my past, so why are my thoughts circling that wagon. I was wondering, am I still that weak naïve little girl at age 13, trading one Hell for another, domestic violence that I never had the strength to deal with because the battle inside of my head was too much for me to handle. That decision lead me into being angry, depressed and at times to go into seclusion within myself. I lost myself as a woman, but I never allowed it to affect my sons. Being positive, compassionate and loving was my method of raising them.

The morning came fast, and sleep had evaded me because all my fears were flooding back front and center. I laid in bed until 1PM, frozen, I didn't answer my phone or talked to anyone. When I finally got up,

I moved in slow motion and the tears were nonstop. As I dressed for work, I moved in slow motion and I could barely bring myself to touch my body or look in the mirror to see this broken girl. When I got to my car, I gave myself the speech what I normally did when life got a little difficult. The crazy thing was that I didn't have faith in my speech this time, it was just me hiding within myself. As I pulled into work, I said to myself, girl pull it together, you are strong, and nothing can shake you. When I entered the building to clock in, someone immediately asked; what's wrong with you? I lost it in front of everyone. My head started hurting again and the voices were not making any sense. Everyone had an opinion about what was going on in my body and telling me that I would be okay. Then a friend looked at me and I could feel her looking through me to my soul, it hurt deep within. The tears would not stop, and I could not find any peace and I didn't know if it would ever be peaceful for me again. After work, I drove home completely numb but I couldn't seem to get out of my car. It took me an hour to get out of my car and make it upstairs because I felt that I was going back to the place where my life had changed and where I had found the lump in my breast.

    I undressed slowly, reminding myself not to touch that side of my body. The water was extremely hot running on my body and then it happened again, the headache came, and I lost my balance. He was on top of me, saying you did this to yourself for being so beautiful that I had to have you. I don't know how long I was out or how long he was on top of me. I wanted to scream but nothing came out of my mouth. I wanted cry and ask him why you are inside of me, but his body was too much for me to bare. He was in my ear saying how he always loved me. The smell of him burned my eyes. I looked at him trying to focus on who this man was, his voice sounded familiar. Then I turned cold and sick on the inside because I remembered the secret that I was carrying, I was pregnant at age of 17 and scared. His voice was killing me slowly on the inside to the point that I couldn't focus on how I was naked without taking my clothes off. The last thing I remembered was being in my boyfriend's stepfather's car because he was bringing me from West Palm Beach, Florida to Orlando. Then I remember, he had given me something to drink, a bottle of water. Now, I was back in the shower where the water was so hot, and my skin was extremely red from scrubbing, but I couldn't move to turn the water off. After the shower, I made it to my bed and sat thinking to myself, I don't want to die, what about my sons and grandbaby whom I had fallen in love with. Thinking to myself, I must make a very hard decision and that meant fighting and never giving up on myself.

    A new day has begun, I woke up at 5AM and made the decision not to wait for the two months for my doctor's appointment. I showered, got dressed and drove to Spectrum Hospital where they saw walk-in patients. The awkward thing was I couldn't bring myself to get out of my car. I turned on the music and pulled out a book to read. I looked at the clock and it was 1PM, I had parked there at 9AM, I had not moved one inch. My mind was a basket case, so I started my speech to myself, got out of the card, walk don't cry, and you can't give up. I talked to myself which is very effective; Hahaha for forty years now. I know it sound crazy, but it keeps me whole and focused, that was the only way I knew. Once inside the building, my appointment was scheduled at Holland Hospital, 8AM Monday morning.

    That was the longest weekend of my life, I didn't eat or sleep, and mostly I stayed in my room and cried. I couldn't tell my children because I needed to know the damage. I wanted to protect them. Monday was sunny, a new journey for me had begun. The appointment was crazy, as I was walking into the building, I slipped and went right on my knees. An older gentleman helped me up and assisted me to the door. I had a female doctor which relaxed me a little, she made me feel comfortable and I trusted her the moment we met. All the necessary test was completed with a return appointment on the following Tuesday for the breast biopsy. I knew my findings would be Cancer. I started having massive headache with vision loss and vomiting where I couldn't walk. I was not functional, but I still could not let my children know what was going on with my health.

When it was time for the biopsy results, I asked my girlfriend to accompany me. This was the hardest thing that I had to do in my life, to ask someone to be there for me. Her agreeing to be there for me didn't prepare me for her insane mind frame, she is crazy, crazy. There are reasons why I choose her to be with me is because I didn't want to lose myself and I wanted laughter at the end of this journey. To see the humor in my life has always been the key to my health and in raising my children.

The morning of the test results took me back to my past again where I was that little girl trying to find answers to what did I do to my mom? We entered the building and I had a change of mind, but my girlfriend pushed me in the door. As I suspected, the result was Stage 2 Breast Cancer, which meant surgery to remove the tumor, then chemotherapy and radiation. Hearing that news was different than me knowing it. Immediately, I ran to the lady's room and I fell to the floor to vomit and try to disappear because I couldn't breathe, what was I going to tell my children? I looked in the mirror and called on my faith that has always guided me since I was six years old. I asked whatever road you chose me to go, I will understand but please teach me how to forgive from my soul to let things go. When I got off the floor, I pulled up my big girl panties, opened the door and told myself, you are allowed to scream, laugh and say whatever you are feeling but you are not allowed to be silent. I knew when I opened that door my girlfriend would be standing right there waiting on me. The surgery date was December 22, 2106, to remove the cancer and to find out if it had spread or if I had the gene. The decision was made but I did try to push it back because of the fear of the unknown and now I had to tell my children.

I was extremely tense leaving the doctor's office, heading to see my children to deliver the news about me having breast cancer. They looked at me and asked if I was in any pain, then they said my chances were extremely high with treatment. I was so proud of them with their positive attitudes and outlook, this is how I had raised them. This was better than I expected, I never wanted to cause them any type of pain. My next decision was to put my diagnosis on Social Media all my friends, women and men. This was a way of breaking the silence within me, I have always stayed silent and closed off. I asked my friends to come to the hospital with positive energy and laugher because laughter heals the soul. When the day came to remove the tumor, a lot of my amazing friends and my children came to support me with the humor I requested. The tumor was 5.2 centimeters larger than what was expected which meant I was definitely having chemotherapy and radiation. Once the cancer was removed, the headaches stopped, and my lymph nodes were negative. This was great news to receive right before Christmas. Glory to God, God is Amazing!

On the day of chemotherapy, my youngest son went with me for the treatment, he has my crazy, goofy sense of humor. A couple of my girlfriends accompanied me also. The regime to prepare yourself for treatment horrendous, to be stabbed in your chest was crazy. I would wake up four hours early before my appointment to numb my chest, but the pain was deadly. The second day after treatment was horrific; vomiting, sweats, exhaustion and nausea which debilitated me to the point that I wanted to stop the treatment. I lost all of my beautiful hair. My oldest son was amazing, he took my tears and turned them into laughter. I couldn't look at myself in a mirror or touch my body because of the scars on my body. The one thing that was hard for me was losing friends because I have cancer, they wouldn't call, text or hang out with me. That bothered me because cancer was not my fault, it made me feel rejected like I did with my parents. It came to the point that I didn't want to get out of bed except for work because of depression. I felt like I was dying on the inside with no fight in me. I wouldn't let anyone see my weakness or pain because I didn't want anyone to pity this girl who was known to be strong and a fighter. This behavior didn't last very long because I was reliving my past at the same time I was literally fighting for my life. I realized I was losing my identity again as when I was a child or in a relationship. I started remembering buying food because of being homeless and hungry. The memory came back as I stood with a cart filled with food standing in the store, this was after my second treatment. I left the cart in the middle of the store and walked out, got in my car and drove to Grandville before I realized that I was looking for a place to end my life, I was so overwhelmed with memories.

I sat in the mall parking lot in Grandville for two hours contemplating on taking my life, I went over every detail of me as a mother and as a woman. I recited my prayer for strength not to ever give up on me and to teach me how to forgive myself, to forgive others but most of all to let go of things that are out of my control that doesn't give me peace. (Mark 11:25-26)

My soul felt so heavy. I called my children, but I didn't tell them I was really lost. It was then that I choose to be compassionate and thankful about the life that I was given.

I went home and made two list of what I wanted to do to because I needed to start healing. One list was of silly things that I wanted to do, the other list was my passion. I called some girlfriends that love my goofy behavior to let them know which weekends movies were, plays, comedy shows or just dinner. I started loving to live, to open up about my life. I also am learning to forgive starting with things I have no control over. Cancer triggered my past memory of hell but has set me on a journey of forgiveness. (Isaiah 53:5)

Dr. Cynthia J. Hines

PUT A NAME ON IT

Loss of life is necessary, for new life to begin. Jesus had to ascend to heaven, so the Comforter could come. Even though Jesus' disciples were saddened by His departure, it was necessary. Likewise, it is necessary to work through the layers of emotion that accompany death to reach a new normal. With a new normal comes a new assignment which provides new knowledge and experience which can lead to spiritual growth if you're open to the process. There is a benefit to be received when you are open and learn to on God 100% and Him alone. Most importantly, you gain a fresh testimony and anointing that others can see and feel as you describe the goodness of the Lord. When you have a fresh testimony, you speak with a greater conviction. The conviction in your heart has the power to touch another heart. Another heart that is hurting and has yet to heal. <u>We must find that new normal because life will NEVER be the same; it is necessary.</u>

I wanted to share a personal story that would resonate with people and have the power to heal. *Put a Name on It* is the story about my mother's transition to glory on December 25th. I have heard many times that losing your mother is unlike any other experience. Friends and others told me that it could take years before you feel like yourself once again. The feeling of not being yourself, is indescribable.

As a co-pastor with my husband in Riverview, Michigan we have comforted many bereaved families. My Bishop at my home church would even call upon me to pray nearly every Mother's Day to strengthen those whose mothers were no longer alive. When my mother passed my biggest my biggest struggle, was the over whelming sense of helplessness. I wanted so desperately to get a handle on my emotions, to be a big girl, to get over it. After all, I'm supposed to know how to respond in these situations, right? The sense of a total loss of control is unnerving. Even though we say we trust God, finding yourself in a state of "free fall" will surely test your faith. When I started this journey, I had so many questions. Answers were extremely difficult to find and even slower to come. I mean REAL answers, answers that resonated with me, answers that sounded like what I was experiencing. I wondered "Am I normal? Will, I ever get better? How long will it take before I feel like myself again?

My biggest barrier to healing was words. I could not find the words to describe my feelings without sounding crazy or, so I thought. I simply could not, *Put a Name on It*. I found that there were layers to my emotion. Every time I would say to myself, I'm getting better, my grief would manifest itself in an unusual way. A form I had never seen before, another layer of hurt. I discovered that digging through the layers of emotion is an evolutionary process. Although you are digging deep inside your emotions, interesting learnings about yourself begin to surface; a new you starts to evolve. However, digging through the layers requires work. The work can be difficult, unpleasant and slow. The work is called grief work. Jesus was a man that experienced grief and knew what it meant to be sorrowful.

... A man of sorrows,
and acquainted with grief....
Isaiah 53:3

Jesus knows our struggle and He's ready and willing to help us work our way back. If you neglect yourself and skip grief work you can become stuck. There are few things more frustrating than being stuck. *When you know you are stuck*, a new wave of anxiety hits which can delay your recovery. You can become suspended between layers and believe that you *are* better since you have resumed normal activities such as work, school or chores at home. However, beneath the surface there could be emotions which lay in wait for the most inopportune time to spring forth. You could be one wrong word from lashing out unprovoked. One dreadful day at work from your alienating your co-workers. A pin prick away from a complete meltdown. Do not be surprised if you are not fully healed because you skipped grief work. Listed below are central questions often associated with grief. I believe many people privately ponder these questions more.

AM I NORMAL?

Most likely yes, it is natural to wonder if your feelings are normal. You only have one mother and there's no way to predict how you will respond to such a loss. Even if you previously lost a parent each incident is different. Each parent and your relationship with them is unique. It is normal to cry and cry a lot. Often, we try to fight back the tears for fear of appearing weak or unstable. The bible says that "Jesus wept" when His friend Lazarus died. You are not exempt from those same emotions; man or woman. In addition to tears, sleeping more is also a common response to grief. You could be very fatigued after a long hospitalization, funeral and many visitors. You will need time to recuperate and adjust. Taking care of your mother's affairs after she has passed can seem overwhelming emotionally and physically. In the Garden of Gethsemane, Jesus attempted to wake the disciples three times as the time for His death was approaching. The bible says the disciples' eyes were very heavy. When we are sad, grieving or feel a sense of heaviness sleeping can be a coping mechanism when life becomes too much. When my father passed nearly 30 years ago, I recall sleeping almost the entire weekend when I came for the funeral.

Rest is essential even though this may sound overly simple. However, I found that even months after the funeral my energy level was not the same as before my mother's passing. Many people told me to "take it easy". I thought what do they mean by take it easy? Obviously, I plan to sleep at night and I might take a nap during the day. However, I realized I needed to lighten my schedule. Cut back on planned activities so that if your body tells you to rest you can. Often, as women we over load our schedules. However, if Superwoman loses her mother, please take time out to rest it's worth it. Listen to your body and cut your schedule to 70 or 80% of what's normal for you.

"and ye shall find rest unto your souls...."
Matthew 11:29

Will, I ever get better?

Yes, with God all things are possible; yet every case is unique. The strength of the relationship with your mother is one important factor. For example, my mother and I were extremely close. My siblings never lived in the house when I was growing up, so it was the two of us. For example, most holidays revolved around my mother for me.

Mostly recently I was not looking forward to Mother's Day. Typically, on Mother's Day we would be together the entire day starting with church. All the children and grandchildren would come to church; even those that do not regularly attend. Frequently we would take family pictures in color coordinated outfits with all four generations. Dinner meant Mother's Day Brunch at the Holiday Inn in the ballroom a 20-year family tradition. This year will be the first without her and I have literal planned for months how I would survive the day without a meltdown. I got through the day but with a major sinus headache. My body has been under physical attack from one aliment to another although the issues seem unrelated.

Also, your healing in large part depends on you. Your capacity, your resilience, your spirituality and faith. Your willingness, to dig through the layers of emotions you feel even though you would rather have a root canal. God wants you to trust the process and His ability to restore your heart, He is the great physician.

Planning certainly helps; by thinking ahead about days, places or situations that could trigger your grief you'll be better prepared for any rush of emotion. If you know you are not "ready" for a situation do not push it. Bow out graceful and give your recovery more time. My birthday was a couple of months ago and I knew I would miss my mom that day. Usually around 8 a.m., she would call me because that was close to the time I born. She would make a special effort to celebrate our birthdays. I knew my birthday would be rough, so I planned a very relaxing day. I had a manicure, pedicure, eyebrows arched, my husband took me shopping and we had dinner at an upscale restaurant with close friends. Did I shed tears on my birthday? Absolutely, but nothing like one might expect. Overall, I had a very nice and memorable day.

> *"**For** I know the thoughts that I think toward you, saith the Lord"*
> *Jeremiah 29:11*

How long will it take before I feel like myself?
I wish I could tell you how long it will take to feel like yourself. It will take the time that it takes.

I asked many people this question in search of a comforting response. When I spoke with others that lost their mothers, the time frames ranged from eighteen months to twenty years. I rebuked that spirit that said 20 years. The challenge is things will NEVER be the same. I have to learn to be ok with that fact. This is an extremely scary and sometimes depressing thought. Usually we say, "I'll be glad when things get back to normal". Each grieving person must discover their new normal to move forward. Initially I could not find my new normal because I ***did not want to move forward.*** It may sound strange, but I did not what move forward ***without her.*** I was waiting to wake up from this nightmare. I did not want to "forget" her. She was too important; how could I leave her behind? I needed to find a way to bring her along with me.

Over a year prior to my mom's death we traveled to Mississippi the two of us for my 98-year-old Aunt's funeral. I felt the trip would likely be my mother's last opportunity to travel south. My mother would now be the oldest family member at 95 years old. Our flight south departed from Detroit. I thought that since our flight departed at 6 a.m. not many people would be traveling that early on a weekday. Wrong, it was Spring Break and airport was packed to capacity. I asked our airport attendant to take my mother to the departure gate in her wheelchair while I checked our luggage. Due to the very long lines and chaos in the airport, I was unable to get through security on time. I was totally distraught. Because I was told my mother made the flight which had departed. I stood silent at the ticket counter with tears dripping from my face. The desk attendant that had been extremely rude saw my face. She must have felt sorry for me because her entire disposition changed. She rebooked me on the next flight.

Eventually, I got through security and slowly walked to the gate. As I approached the gate I blinked my eyes as if I was seeing things. My mother was sitting in her wheelchair with the attendant at the gate. I said, "I thought you were gone?" She started to giggle as she often did when she knew she had caused trouble. She was also laughing because she knew I had been crying. I said, mom they told me you were on the plane. She said, "Nope, I told the pilot I can't leave without my daughter." She said the pilot looked at her several times before departing as if she did not understand the plane was leaving. My mother was giggling, she thought it was so funny. I shook my head and said, what was I thinking?

I forget who my mother was, I should have **known** that no one makes her do ANYTHING. She tells YOU what she's going to do.

Just like that day when I thought we were separated, my head knows the truth, but my heart is not listening. My heart does not want to leave her behind today any more than I did that day. But God ….

> "The troubles of my heart are enlarged:
> O bring thou me out of my distresses"
> Psalm 25:17

Many people will freely share their story about their mother's transition. However, It is evident that many of them are not totally healed. You can see the repressed grief in their eyes and their continence. Most times people are content to just survive the situation. They try to simply outlive the pain, make it through the situation with the least amount of pain. While it may be counter intuitive to embrace your pain, I discovered that my pain is the path to peace.

While a peaceful state feels much better than pain, it is not the destination. Peace is a plateau, a place of rest if you need it, but peace cannot last with complete restoration. If you stay on the peace plateau too long, you could become complacent and forget you unfinished work. Progress is ultimately where God wants us to be. It may be unthinkable, that life could be richer without mother. I can barely speak it; the words sound like blasphemy rolling off my lips. Yes, things will NEVER be the same, but God does not want you to be the same, He wants you to be BETTER. Better for the experience, better from a closer walk with Him. The same is no longer good enough. The continuum of *PAIN, PEACE* and *PROGRESS* is a formula for total healing. If you stop at peace you will fail to soar, your healing is incomplete. God revealed to me that my Mother had poured EVERYTHING into me that God gave her. Now it is time for her to rest from labor and time for me to soar like never before.

Storytelling can be very powerful, as you share fond memories of your mother with friends and family often. The fact that you can tell stories, is a sign of recovery. Even if you become teary while storytelling, you can experience her warmth as when she was with you. That warmth is a signal that your mother is not left behind. You carry her spirit in your heart. My cousin that lost his mother, the Aunt in Mississippi, told me "When I started to remember the good times with mom, that's when I got my breakthrough." I have held onto that advice and it has helped me tremendously. When my children visit we laugh out loud at my mother's famous sayings. We laugh when we catch ourselves channeling our inner mama or gran as they call her. Instead of suppressing your grief, work through it and find a way to laugh.

"Shew me thy ways, O Lord; teach me thy paths.
Lead me in thy truth, and teach me: for thou art the God of my salvation;
on thee do I wait all the day"
Psalm 25:4-5

Put a Name on It, seeks to help you to understand your feelings and lean into you feeling. What you are feeling is natural. By leaning in rather the resisting you facilitate your recovery with God's help. Even though it was difficult, I created a list below of layers to approximate my journey and where I stand today to help someone else. I am still trusting God for total healing. I am poised to soar in Jesus name. Amen!

THE LAYERS

Aching - the first most unpleasant stage. This layer will feel the most extreme and uncomfortable. After a significant loss its normal to feel despair, depression, sadness, anxiety, uncontrolled weeping, short tempered, gut wrenching anxiety. My heart physically hurt at times. I grew weary of people saying I'm sorry for your loss. At times I felt I was making it through the day fine until ten people reminded that I had a great lost. They would then start to share their story. People are well intended, but many times they do not know what to say, so expect it and perhaps limit your exposure if possible. (1 month)

Struggling – during this stage I experienced listlessness, lack of interest in normal activities, fatigue, low energy, unable to concentrate, easy to cry, teary eyed. Simple tasks at times seemed over whelming such as cooking, house cleaning or going to the store. This stage is why I recommended a scaled back schedule to 70-80%. It's not unusual if you do not operate at your previous capacity (2 to 3 months)

Surviving – while you may feel considerably better, with much less crying, it's not uncommon to think about mom every day. I found this surprising because I'm not sure that I thought about her every day when she was alive? Perhaps I did but never noticed. You may have limited ability to function, and thereby need to limit the time span for activities. Don't overdo it or push yourself. You may still avoid certain situations that might make you sad such as funerals. Some people self-medicate to combat depression by using a vice such as drugs, alcohol or sex. My vice has always been food. I also developed a strong need to see my family more often, my grandchildren lifted my spirit. I was functioning better on the surface but with a lack of self-control when it came to food plus no exercise. (Month 3-4)

Thriving - a turning point for me was I made a conscious decision to move forward. Much less crying but still occasionally. I decided to Get My Fight Back. I developed a food plan, started journaling what I ate to hold myself accountable. I bought a bike, so I could ride outside rather than exercise in a gym. I tried to be more intentional to the things that make me feel pampered. Take care of my nails, hair, and weight, eat healthy, exercise and get more sleep. Sleep is essential to your mental, emotional and physical health. I almost forgot to say prayer. Shortly after the funeral I started praying 5 weekdays at 7am with two very close friends. I thank God for them at this time of my life, it has been the best decision. We never miss! This is my journey, it's not rocket science but its working for me and I thank the Lord for healing. (Month 5 and counting)

Shonquil "Shonny" Jones Dyson

THE SETBACK THAT BECAME THE SETUP

THE DREAM

I've always wanted to have a family that I could depend on. Being able to trust the ones you love is one of the most important things in a relationship. I thought for sure that the perfect family is precisely what I had. By the time I was twenty-two, I was married to my high school sweetheart and became the mother of a beautiful baby girl. My husband held down two jobs to take care of us. I always kept a job; however, I never made as much. Through the years, we managed to make huge strides together. The Lord blessed us to buy a home, and at that time, we had two children and great jobs at the hospital.

As a child, I carried the desire to be successful. I wanted to be a writer and a singer. I had always imagined myself in the spotlight helping people. Life took a different turn, and that didn't happen for me as I'd envisioned, but I was still content with my little family.

I enjoyed watching my children grow and sprout into these little independent people. While thinking everything was simply perfect, life happened. There was a shake in my marriage that caused me to doubt myself. No, it wasn't an affair, but it was just as bad. It was a connection that tore down my confidence and had me question everything about myself.

I spent five years fighting depression and missing out on family time with my children. I managed to lose myself in being everything for everyone around me. I forgot who I was and what I wanted out of life. I had grown used to settling. I had gotten used to my husband paying bills and running the business of the household. I didn't know anything about going to pay utilities or managing money. I didn't worry about keeping the laundry maintained or cooking dinner. My husband managed to handle it all. I would ask him if there was anything that I could do and he'd always tell me he was fine and everything was okay. Later, I found out we were draining each other. I wanted more, and he wanted less, but neither of us said anything.

Don't get me wrong; I did have my share of duties in our home. Even though it wasn't a worry to cook dinner, I still made sure we ate every day. I also ensured the kids had everything they needed. I worked and kept a full-time job. My father was ill during the first half of my marriage, and I was his caregiver. I made sure his bills were paid and everything else he needed, I managed to take care of it.

The fact that I was taking care of my dad and our kids was one of the reasons my husband helped a lot in keeping our home together. On the flip side, he was also assisting his family with his sick grandmother. So, here you have two young adults trying to have a successful marriage and raise children and take care of sick family members. It was all too much and we failed to realize where the stress and strain was coming from.

After nine years of marriage, I started noticing a change in my home. Tension and discord started to take root, and the peace that I had grown accustomed to begin to vanish. My spouse started to find entertainment elsewhere. He grew to love motorcycles and hanging out during late hours. Anytime he wanted to get away; he'd just jump on his bike and take a ride. Our time together became less and less, and our tolerance became shorter and smaller.

The times that I needed him, he was not around. My calls were ignored and so was my presence. It was like I was living with a stranger. My heart was broken. The strong hugs and sweet words turned into the complete opposite. The man that was my everything became irritated and annoyed with me. I was accused of being boring and not having any interest outside of my family. Yes, I had goals and desires, but I had young children, and I wanted to be available while they were young. I was okay with placing my dreams aside and waiting for the children to get older. I knew that God would supply and provide another chance for me to fulfill my destiny.

So be strong and courageous! Do not be afraid and do not panic before them. For the Lord your God will personally go ahead of you. He will neither fail you nor abandon you.
Deuteronomy 31:6 (NLT)

May the God who gives endurance and encouragement give you the same attitude of mind toward each other that Christ Jesus had, so that with one mind and one voice you may glorify the God and Father of our Lord Jesus Christ.
Romans 15:5-6 (NIV)

BROKEN PROMISE: THE SETBACK

The promise to love, honor and obey was my favorite part of our vows. I thought those words were the glue for a successful marriage. I would never have imagined in a million years that the man I once loved would dislike me so much. I can say we tried and I could tell that he loved me. I also could tell that he was fighting with some decisions that he had to make at this point of his life. I was scared, angry and disappointed all at once. I didn't know how to make it better. I prayed, fasted, and we went to counseling, but nothing seemed to work. I knew for sure that it was an attack of the enemy trying to break my family. I also couldn't help but think God was maybe trying to shift my focus.

I had always had others take care of me. I didn't have to worry about anything. I was favored, and it showed. The stress and strain on my marriage soon took a toll on both my husband and I. We eventually started to avoid each other. I understood that ministry began at home and at that time in my life, my focus was my family. As my fairytale slowly turned into a nightmare, I cried out to God, asking what I must do to save my family. I wanted to know what I needed to do to avoid being everything my haters wanted me to be. I was tired of living in a situation that made me feel less than my value. I found the strength to move out. I got my kids, and I left. I moved out of the way so that God could work. I realized I couldn't fix it. I had to let go and let God.

FAITH DON'T FAIL ME NOW

New apartment. New responsibility. I was in my place with my children. I instantly leaped into overseeing and making sure the bills were paid, and that food and clothes were provided. I was so afraid because I had limited survival skills. I had no idea of how to manage money and get business taken care of. I was terrified. On top of all the changes in my life, my prayer life took a wrong turn. Right when I should have been fasting and praying the most, my faith began to slip.

I started to miss church services; I gave up serving in music ministry, and I spent more time doing other things to keep myself busy. My friend circle began to change, and those who had known me forever started to notice the negative shift I had made. I felt like I had one foot in and the other out. My soul wanted to cling to God, but my flesh wanted instant gratification. I started acting out in ways I had never experienced before. Wine quenched my thirst for rest and slowly, other things started creeping in. I realized I had allowed my situation to change me in a way I despised. I had backslid.

For the righteous falls seven times and rises again, but the wicked stumble in times of calamity. Do not rejoice when your enemy falls, and let not your heart be glad when he stumbles, lest the Lord see it and be displeased, and turn away his anger from him.
Proverbs 24:16-18 (ESV)

NOT DEAD, MERELY ASLEEP: THE SETUP

Meanwhile, all the people were wailing and mourning for her. "Stop wailing," Jesus said. "She is not dead but asleep."
Luke 8:52 (NIV)

Sometimes the beginning seems like the end. The topsy-turvy way the spectrum of a life can spiral out of what seems like "control" is quite bewildering! - Ida West

The idea of mending my marriage seemed far-fetched. I gave up on the dream of writing and ministry. I felt that since I had fallen, it was impossible because I was indeed unworthy. People became comfortable with the idea that I was in a low place. They laughed behind my back, but what they didn't know was there was still a little fuel in my fire. I had tried to put the ideas to rest, but then something happened. It's like out of nowhere, my past prayers were being answered. My fears of being able to provide for my kids vanished.

God had opened doors where I got a raise on my job, and I could even purchase my first car off the lot with a payment I could easily afford. God also made it possible for me to pay for classes out of pocket for billing and coding so that I may get an even better job after graduation.

Things started to look up for me. All those negative words that were spoken over my life began to fall out. The relationship between my husband and I began to get better. We started noticing that time away brought us closer. It was as if the time I had spent going through hard times was preparing me for the rest of my life. My dreams started to show color again. God sent people into my life who spoke power into my destiny. They gave me strength and encouragement when I thought it was over. That second chance to fulfill my destiny came back around. New life was blooming in my future, and that which many hoped was dead still had life.

Throw off your old sinful nature and your former way of life, which is corrupted by lust and deception. Instead, let the Spirit renew your thoughts and attitudes. Put on your new nature, created to be like God truly righteous and holy.
Ephesians 4:22-24 The Holy Bible NIV

FIGHT BACK!

When I was in the middle of my problems, I thought that my life was over. I didn't see any light at the end of the tunnel. Though it was a hard lesson to learn, I now thank God for it. Yes, my spouse and I separated, and everything I thought was my future foundation was wiped out. Even with all these, it was still for my good.

Don't lay down and die with the very thing that is weighing you down. Get up and fight. I kept people around who didn't care about the details of me and my spouse; they cared about what God had in His plans for us. Intercessors that prayed for me when I couldn't pray for myself is what kept me going. I learned how to listen to my heart. I learned how to be a well-rounded person and the strength that was dying within, because I was comfortable, is now stronger than ever. The very thing that hurts can also be the thing that pushes you to your greater self. Yes, change is different and quite scary, but you can do it.

For God has not given us a spirit of fear, but of power and of love and of a sound mind. (2 Timothy 1:7; NKJV)

God will not leave you. He didn't leave me; I turned my back when it got too hard. Don't let that be your story, but if it should happen, repent. Get right with God and trust His plan. I've gone through the loss of a parent, clinical depression, and separation. For some people, one of those three things would have broken them. I thank God for every trial and test because even with the setback, my comeback was more powerful.

My story is nothing but God. I could've lost my mind, but God saw fit to bring me to a place in my life where I can do what I love and provide for my family. I may not be a superstar, and my dreams of fame haven't come true just yet, but I believe God and I want everything He promised. Don't let the enemy trick you out of your inheritance. Marriage is hard, but it is a blessing when God is in control. Raising a family and taking care of sick family can be a strain on any relationship.

Don't play the blame game; fight for your family. Every situation is different. There will be good advice and some bad, but continue to pray, and I promise, God will lead you to the right path. God is still God, even when things look impossible.

KEEP FIGHTING:

- Prayer is the key.
- Don't lose your faith.
- Don't pray and worry—one cancels out the other. It's impossible to be successful in both.
- Know that God loves you and even in tough times, He is still there.

- When you fall, don't let pride keep you down too long. We are harder on ourselves more than anything. Forgive like God forgives.
- Be patient. Have faith and watch the Lord work.

To live a perfect life is impossible. Striving to do so is applauded. Be blessed.

JacQuaye A. Payne

"I AM ONE PERSON" FIGHT FOR YOUR RIGHT TO BE YOU

If you've had the opportunity to read volumes I and II of "A Next Level Shift", then you're well aware of the principles that we, as authors, try to impart within our readers. Whether sharing testimonies of faithlessness to hope, tragedy to triumph, shame to honor, or abuse to love; both books ultimately give a glimpse into how God orchestrated a change in the individual lives of each author. I am one of dozens of women testifying of God's goodness with the intent to simply encourage others that God also has a plan for you... even when you can't see it, feel it, believe it, touch it, or envision it!

In brief, I previously shared how I battled with low self-esteem due to a series of choices I'd made, along with various life events, which landed me in some unfavorable situations such as pregnancy, homelessness, and emotional abuse. I also shared how I suffered from years of thinking I was worthless, unwanted, and undeserving. As a result, I was left in a state of paralysis, completely unable to move forward because I was too broken to believe in myself any longer.

One thing I've learned along my journey; however, is the importance of understanding that **I Am One Person**. And while this is not an incredibly profound or prolific realization, it's true! Why is this relevant you might ask? Well, in our society, we define ourselves in general concepts and broad statements, often determined by outside factors, which doesn't give room for the individuality that God has created us in.

Take for instance the statements, "I am a woman," or "I am a student." The generalization is that if I am a woman I should know how to cook, I want to have children, and that I naturally desire marriage. If I'm a student, I get good grades and I'm diligent about my studies because I desire a good life which can only be attained through education. But what happens if I don't know how to cook, I don't desire to be a mother or wife, or I'm a student struggling with poor grades?

Society dictates that I'm not operating to my optimized capacity or some other stereotype (such as the gender role of a woman) and in turn, I internalize who I am and where I am in my life as feelings of inadequacy, failure, or shame! The end result sounds something like this in our minds: "I'll never be good enough for my family because I don't measure up to my sister who has it all; the husband, kids, and career." Perhaps that internal voice sounds like this: "I don't see anyone else struggling this much in class! If I don't buckle down, I can lose my scholarships! Why can't I just do better?"

To put it in relevant terms, what if I profess to be a Christian, but I struggle with smoking or I can't seem to get rid of feelings of desiring the intimacy of a man? I know I should not have called him over at 2:00 a.m., but he's on his way now and I'm well aware of what will happen once he arrives (and truthfully, I don't want to stop it).

What about if I struggle to read the Bible because it's not that interesting and I really find it difficult to pray without ceasing because it feels like I'm talking to thin air? Have I seriously not measured up to the standard of success as a woman, good student *or* Christian all because the path that I'm on doesn't look like where someone else believes I should be? Am I not successful because I struggle at being perfect 100% of the time?

I often ask, "What is the backstory," because one always exists. Perhaps that woman saw examples of broken women in her life who were solely dependent on men. Maybe she grew up thinking that she simply wanted to be fulfilled by her terms; established both personally and professionally and with a wholeness of self, before she opened up her heart to a man or started a family. In comparison to other women and societal standards; however, she has now internalized her goals of fulfillment as not adding up to success as a woman.

Perhaps the reason that student is struggling is because he's the sole financial supporter for his siblings and ill parent, so working third shift is the only way to pay the bills while attending school full-time during the day. He knows that he's got a lot on his plate which prevents him from getting the good grades he desires, but he still compares himself to his fellow classmates who have less responsibility at 20 years old. Instead of acknowledging his very own persistence to push beyond his heavy burdened tasks, he looks down upon himself because of what he's internalized; perhaps from professors or other outside messages, telling him that he's not applying himself or taking school seriously.

Oh and that Christian. That unworthy and sinful Christian! How dare she not be perfect from the time she accepted Jesus Christ as her personal Savior! How dare she struggle with tobacco addiction or fornication! If she was truly committed to Jesus then she wouldn't give into fleshly temptation, right? Perhaps she wasn't really saved after all!

Or at least, these are some of the unrealistic standards *church folks* put on their fellow sisters and brothers in Christ. Galatians 5:17 tells us, "For the flesh desires what is contrary to the Spirit, and the Spirit what is contrary to the flesh. They are in conflict with each other, so that you are not to do whatever you want." For whatever reason, we often allow outsider's narratives to define us; as unworthy of God's love because fleshly desires seem to rise up, instead of acknowledging that we are on a journey of growth.

The reality is this: I desire to be right in God's eyes, and although I might have given into my own desire and missed the mark this time, I will fight even harder to hit the mark next time, and God still loves me even when I make errors.

Now getting back to my point of understanding that **I Am One Person**. Generalizing oneself is limiting in that, if we find ourselves outside the parameters of the generalization, it becomes incredibly difficult to bypass the idea of what's normal or accepted, thus we fault and label ourselves as not good enough. This makes it more difficult to maintain our identity.

Simply put, you'll never be able to fit a circle into a square hole and if you try to make it fit, there are going to be some disadvantages to pushing against what exists. There's going to be a natural resistance when you're tightly squeezed, confined, bent and reshaped into something you're not. In some cases, you might even have to lose some parts of yourself in order to fit because your circle is too big for the square you were never destined to be shaped into. And the end result is certain to be uncomfortable, that is, loss of your identity, loss of faith, loss or hope, or loss of direction.

So what does this all mean? In layman's terms, you are an individual with many different layers, gifts, talents, and dreams who can't be boxed in or described by general standards because God didn't make you that way. God created man in His own image, in the image of God He created him; male and female He created them (Genesis 1:27). God is multi-faceted, loving, caring, and cannot be boxed in, and neither can you because you're made in his image!

The standard we should follow is God's true standard which is far above and different from that of society or man's interpretation. And within the image that God created us, God has also given us each an individual identity, calling, and assignment on our lives. The deceit of the enemy; however, is to prevent us from seeing who God formed us to be and dismantling our true knowledge of self.

Take me for instance: I had gone through four years of college and graduated cum laude, having received my Bachelor of Arts (B.A.) degree in Communications and Marketing by age 21. I then decided to go back to school with the goal of obtaining my Master of Business Administration (M.B.A.) degree by 27. I surpassed that personal goal and graduated on my 26th birthday with my M.B.A. in Project Management. The years to come turned into a whirlwind of proving to myself, and others, that I deserved to be in prominent spaces where I could exercise my intellect, accompanied by hopes of income compensation that would provide comfortably for me and my family.

Fast forward 10 years and add on the sting of approximately 500 resumes, cover letters, and applications sent out to employers who claimed to be interested in recruiting talented workers, and not one single attempt landed me what I desired most; a career! My identity was totally wrapped up in obtaining success in a career so much so that, I saw myself as "less than" because I had not yet been hired into a prestigious or lucrative company. There was no recurring paycheck, no benefits package with insurance, paid vacation, a 401(k) retirement plan; nothing at all! And while I was truly happy for my friends who navigated through the waters of life; gaining employment in their respective fields, marrying, having kids, purchasing homes, and taking lavish vacations, I was often left with a void asking, "When will it be my turn?"

During those years, so much of my identity was wrapped up in the credentials I had gained, but I was empty inside with feelings of inadequacy as the only thing I had were certifications enclosed within expensive wooden frames hanging on my walls. The degrees I had worked so hard for weren't really working for me. I placed an insane emphasis on defining myself by my educational progress and when it didn't lead me to anything more than working through temp agencies and other unrelated fields, I was lost! As you can imagine, the standard after college isn't to work dead-end jobs, barely able to make ends meet; so by definition of what a college graduate's level of success should have been, I was failing miserably!

It wasn't truly until I became a part of volume I of "A Next Level Shift" that I had a wakeup call, realizing that my identity wasn't at all tied to any educational acronyms. One day Lady Wells, the visionary behind this movement, emailed authors a mockup of what the front and back covers were going to look like. When I initially saw the covers, I thought about requesting a revision to add "M.B.A." after my name (because truthfully, a couple of my co-authors had "PhD" behind their names and it looked wonderful).

It was in that very moment that I thought about how ridiculous and flawed my thinking had been down through the years! Reason being, I certainly didn't need any degrees to be a part of a book collaboration to talk about how God kept me through some of my most difficult situations and I didn't need an esteemed education to minister to other woman! I no longer desired "B.A.", "M.B.A.", or even "AKA" (my sorority) to define me. The only letters that were important were G-O-D.

The intersectionality of my very being tells me many things about who God has created and called me to be. My married name, Payne, indicates that I am a wife while my maiden name, Jacobs, indicates that I am a daughter, sister, niece, aunt, and so on. The fact that two little people call me mommy indicates that I am a mother. But beyond the surface level, God gives us clear instruction and understanding into what He desires for us and from us as individuals. Here are just a few examples of relevant scriptures:

Romans 8:28
And we know that all things work together for good to them that love God, to them who are the called according to His purpose.

(God desires us to trust Him knowing that things will be good; He also desires for us to know that we are His!)

Romans 8:37
Nay, in all these things we are more than conquerors through Him that loved us.

(God desires for us to know our strength and that we are winners because of who He is in our lives!)

Proverbs 16:3
Commit thy works unto the Lord, and thy thoughts shall be established.

(God desires our commitment and for us to know that He'll guide us!)

Psalms 37:3-5
Trust in the Lord and do good; dwell in the land and enjoy safe pasture. Take delight in the Lord, and He will give you the desires of your heart. Commit your way to the Lord; trust in Him and He will do this:

(God desires, once again, trusting in Him, rejoicing in Him, doing His will, and following His directions and He'll give us what we need… and want!)

Proverbs 3:5-6
Trust in the Lord with all thine heart; and lean not unto thine own understanding. In all thy ways acknowledge Him, and he shall direct thy paths.

(God desires us to be okay with not knowing every step and everything! Put Him first and He'll show us the way!)

I am called, a conqueror, safe, desirable to God who directs me because I am His child and he loves me! I am more than a woman who had a baby out of wedlock or a one-time divorcee; more than an educated woman, mother or wife. I am more than my past failures, current struggles, and future successes! **I Am One Person**, yet all these facets of life and stages are a part of me!

It can be difficult to define the spiritual, physical, personal, or professional parts of self; especially with so much outside noise dictating what is *right* and *normal*. The journey to fully operate in the person who God made us to be is often a daunting task to navigate. But the secret is realizing that you don't have to be perfect all the time while putting your best foot forward most times, in spite of the missteps. Just embrace the many layers of who you are. God accepts you for you and He is waiting for you to do the same of yourself.

Wherever you are in your journey; whether fully locked, loaded and combat ready or struggling to pick up your weapons (the Bible, prayer, and fasting), just remember, **I Am One Person**… and I am God's person, at that! So continue to **Fight For Your Right To Be You** because God has a plan for you!

Biography

JacQuaye, originally from Cleveland, Ohio, resides in West Michigan. She is the wife of Minister BeShaun D. Payne, Sr. and they have two children; Jayda-Monay (10) and BeShaun, Jr. (3). She is a proud alumna of the HBCU, Central State University, having pledged Alpha Kappa Alpha Sorority, Inc. (AKA), earning her B.A. and then M.B.A. from Ursuline College. She is currently a Program Officer at her county's local community foundation. JacQuaye and her family attend Holy Trinity Church of God in Christ under the leadership of Bishop Nathaniel W. Wells, Jr. and Mother Mary Ann Wells. JacQuaye is an advocate for diversity & inclusion and views things with a lens of equity, working as a mentor and community activist. For more information, visit www.JacQuayePayne.com.

References

The Holy Bible: Authorized King James Version. Nashville: Thomas Nelson, Inc., 2001. Print
The Holy Bible: The Amplified Bible. 1987. La Habra, CA: The Lockman Foundation.
NIV Women of Faith Study Bible. Grand Rapids: Zondervan, 2002. Print
BibleGateway.com.

Denise Harris

LADY IN THE PEW

The mind games, the guilt, and the shame. The ultimate hurt, the pain and the blame. To healing, to strength, to restoration and victory. God did it all just for me! I'm the Lady in the *pew*!

As a little girl I was so excited to get to the *pew*, to praise and worship God is what I loved to do. The *pew* was a place where I was free to be me. Oh, how I feared God and loved to be in his presence. As I shifted into adulthood my life began to change, my eyes were enlightened, my God, things seemed so strange.

Lord, as I came through the church doors headed towards the *pew*, I felt like I had stepped into a war zone trying to get to you. I dodged bullets and had to take cover, battling the usher in her white worn shoes, just to get to the cushion of the *pew*. This warfare was real, I was fighting! My armor was so heavy! I couldn't believe I was bound in a place where I should have been free. Those demons that came to church today tried to overtake me.

I sat still in the *pew* wanting nothing but peace: yet there was no one to listen or understand me. Alone, I sat wanting to be heard, but no one said a mumbling word. As I sat there wanting to be seen, just one touch or one hug would have intrinsically changed things. I was confused at what I saw: lying, fakeness, love, manipulation, gossip, backbiting, so much sin. I didn't want to be judgmental I just wanted to feel the love of God stirring within. I cried, "Lord, free the existential me of what my natural eyes can physically see, cause if you don't cover them I won't be free." I want to be that lady in the *pew* who sees with spiritual eyes but for the grace of God all those things could have been me. You said in your word to anoint my eyes with eyesalve that I may see. (Rev. 3:18) I'm anointing them Lord, I want to be free!!

I tried to move forward but the weight of the world was sitting on top of me. It was so heavy! I felt buried! I couldn't breathe! I felt like I was suffocating! I asked the Lord to breathe on my bones because they were dry and withered up. I was dying a slow death! I know the bible said to cast my cares on the Lord but really, I didn't know how to trust him. This warfare is intense, I couldn't shake that I messed up last night, I couldn't shake that I wasn't living right, this guilt, this shame is driving me insane. Lord, I'm clinging to the *pew*, I'm here, I showed up but where are you? I'm so lost that I don't know what to do. Clinging to the *pew* is generationally what I knew. Struggling to move, yet afraid to sit still because I knew where I was would not allow my wounds to heal. It would only allow for laughable exposure and infection to set in. Sin on top of Sin!

My God from glory, it was time that I really had to face me; with all my imperfections staring back at me. There I was desperate for change, so I begged; "Lord, please show me, *the me* that you would have me to be; so that I can be free! I'm sitting in this *pew* yearning for more of you, help me to close out the distractions of the world so that I can get my breakthrough. It's time for me to get rid of these old filthy rags and put on my garment of praise."

God heard my cry; he arrested me and held me captive with his amazing love. He began stripping me by pulling off layers and layers of sin. I felt a release and a tugging at my dismembered heart. He was transforming and transitioning me. I began to stand tall and strong like he had ordained for me to be.

In the *pew* I began to rebuild my altar and I went beyond the veil into the inner courts and I allowed for God's supernatural love to shift me into the holy of holies. I was launched into the deep. I became FREE!! Not my will Lord, but thine will be done in me, was my heart's cry.

This freedom caused me to shift into who God had created me to be. Several years later my family and I relocated to a new state and began serving in ministry. I served according to the will of God. I was faithful and I gave all of me. In return, I felt rejected and left alone right in the *pew*; this is where my faith and trust in Jesus grew. My sisters in Christ who I longed to form a Christian relationship with abandoned me. Yes, another church had become another war zone, throwing daggers at me. I continued to show up in full battle rattle, locked and loaded with the word of God. The hurt and rejection had me pondering what I did wrong. Then I realized that when God shifts you to the Next Level you are attacked by different types of devils. Wanting to be a part and wanting to be loved is all I desired. God is love, right? That's what we should do, is love one another. Right? I was so worn out and tired of warring but I realized that the rejection was a place of isolation that God had placed me in so that I could learn to fully commune with Him. I refused to let the enemy win. I would remind myself that the word of God said, "No weapon that is formed against thee shall prosper" and "every tongue that shall rise against thee in judgment thou shalt condemn."(Isaiah 54:17)

I continued to pray for those who plotted against me. I continued to pray for those that smiled in my face but laughed and talked about me behind my back. I refused to fall prey to the tricks of Satan's devices. I knew that the Word of God said: "For we wrestle not against flesh and blood, but against principalities, against powers, against the rulers of the darkness of this world, against spiritual wickedness in high places." (Ephesians 6:12) I was so ready for those high places to come down. Overwhelmed and tired of facing dark opposition. I often wondered how much more I had to endure. Yet, I knew that God wouldn't put any more on me than I could bear but this *Lady in the pew* was ready for the enemy to cease-fire because stress and anxiety was holding me hostage. I know that we should be able to glory in tribulation and *"tribulation worketh patience; and patience, experience; and experience, hope."(Romans 5 3-4)* but this was so stressful. I was in a spiritual drought I was so thirsty and hungry for more of the word of God. I knew my next season was due but how and when was left up to God. For weeks I wailed and called on Jesus. This was my way of counter attacking the enemy. He didn't realize the magnitude of power that comes when you call on the name of Jesus. For weeks I wailed and he finally came in like a flood and ambushed everything. After being on this battlefield for three years and battling in this specific warzone for a little over a year it all ended through a text message. The words "There will be no church service tomorrow if you have any questions contact the Pastor," brought things to a halt. I was attacked by friendly fire. Not only was service cancelled for that day but it was cancelled indefinitely. I had just experienced more church hurt. I couldn't believe after all we had poured into the ministry the doors were closed. Shut down, just like that! Disbelief and devastation would have won but God alone understands why things happened the way that they did!

Why and how did I get here? Not an existential experience but another isolation for a graduation in Christ. Isn't it funny how we pray and ask God for something and when it happens in a different way than what we expect, we have the nerve to trip out about it. At this point I felt like Job, "though he slay me yet will I trust him". In the midst of all of this adversity, I still continue to praise God. I was ready and knew how to fight. God had given me the ability to scan my sector and recognize the tricks of the enemy. I was proactive, I was prayed up, I was seeking His face, I was reading my bible, I was fasting and I was in full armor. I knew that "no weapon formed against me would prosper and that all things worked together for the good, of them that are called according to his purpose." (Romans 8:28) By the grace of God when those fiery darts came the enemy could not touch me, God blocked it. I wore the chinks in my armor like a badge of honor.

Even though we felt like abandoned children that were left on someone's doorstep by their parents, my husband and I found ourselves comforting and consoling others that had just experienced what we did. We received call after call as to what was going on and why the Pastor closed the doors. Not one time did we speak anything negative about the man and woman of God. If any negative conversation started to arise we rerouted the conversation and covered them, not just in conversation but we covered them in prayer. Yes, I was hurt and wrapped up in my emotions, but my spiritual eyes were opened; I could see what Christ was doing. Had the Lord not abruptly shaken things up, my family and I would not have shifted into our next season.

As we shifted we prayed for direction. We prayed for a church home and as my husband would say, "we aren't church hoppers or Holy Ghost Shoppers." We just wanted to be in an authentic ministry that preaches an unadulterated word from heaven, where our spirit man would be free in Jesus to experience miracles, signs and wonders. We decided to google Apostolic Churches in our area and we came across Pastor Cortt Chavis of Truth Chapel Ministries. We listened to one sermon after the next and it turned into an entire day of listening to the word of God. The hunger and thirst that we were yearning for was being filled. The following Sunday we attended church service at Truth Chapel and it became our new church home. To God be the Glory!!!

As I often encounter the *pew* I look back over my life and I thank God for my *experiences* because in the *pew* is where I got my fight back. Fighting according to the word of God, allowed me to focus my attention on the things above which resulted in spiritual revelation and growth. I became the recipient of a Bachelor's degree in General Studies. I became a Co-Author of A Next Level Shift Volume II. I became a Certified Life Coach, as well as a Support and Legal Advocate for Partners Against

Domestic Violence. God also allowed for the birth of A Next Level Girl Talk along with so many more opened doors that allows for me to be a part of the building of his kingdom.

Now I sit like a sponge in desperation, in hope and anticipation of what my Father has in store for me, knowing that no matter what comes my way I will triumph with victory! This *Lady in the Pew* has finally arrived! I'm Soaking in God's presence, free to worship, free to praise God, free to be whom God has predestined me to be!!!!

I want to encourage you and let you know that, if you are that Lady in the *pew* that have been knocked down; get up and dust yourself off because he that begun a good work in you will complete it until the day of Jesus Christ. (Philippians 1:6) Know that it doesn't matter how many times you get knocked down, get up swinging in Jesus Name. God has given you power and authority to whoop the enemy! You can do all things through Christ Jesus who strengthens you. (Philippians 4:13) Honey, God will give you the strength to knock that joker out! Can you say TKO? Yes, Woman of God with the help of the Lord you are victorious because the battle is not yours it's the Lord's and we know the LORD is mighty in battle. "Who is this King of glory? The LORD strong and mighty, the LORD mighty in battle." (Psalm 24:8)

Never underestimate the lady in the *pew* just because she doesn't look like you. She just might be that one that will help pray you through.

Lady in the *pew*, arise God has given you a word, your voice is strong and mighty and needs to be heard. To lift up others and love them back to Christ that's what he did with his ultimate sacrifice.

Lady in the *pew*, the time is now let go of the guilt and the shame, let go of the hurt and the pain; no longer bound you are loosed in Jesus Name.

Lady in the *pew*, if you are discouraged go forth my sister and let your heart become free, from freedom to liberty to victory.

Lady in the *pew*, sitting dormant on your gift due to others not seeing your worth; honey it's time to bind that and give birth! P.U.S.H.

and give birth to the gift that God has given you, because every good and perfect gift is from above. (James 1:17)

Lady in the *pew* that feels unloved or unappreciated, I challenge you to arise my sister and know that God has great things in store for you. "For I know the thoughts that I think toward you, saith the Lord, thoughts of peace, and not of evil, to give you an expected end." (Jeremiah 29:11)

Lady in the *pew*, there is a purpose for your pain, stand tall and fight in Jesus Name!

Lady in the *pew*, let your *pew* experience draw you nearer to God and know that your pew experience is not just for you, it's to help another sister that may be going through.
So if you see a lady sitting in the *pew*: just stop and share a hug or two, you never know what it may do.
Lady in the *pew* find out what works for you: whether it's praying, worshipping, or singing and use that to praise your way through.
Lady in the *pew* it is time that we as women stop looking on the outside to heal the inside when God has already gone before us and prepared a place of peace. We must stop our traditional ways of church in the *pew* and lean on God because his word is true. You can do all things through Christ Jesus who strengthens you! Girl Get your Fight Back!!!

Angela R. Flowers

AS THE SHIFT BEGAN

I was invited by my cousin to do a class with her at our church called "Survival Kit". This was an eight week class. We studied the book of Isaiah, the prophecy that the Messiah was coming as the Savior, to bear the cross and wear a crown. In the book of Isaiah, God lets us know who he is! He tells us in Isaiah 45:5, "I am the Lord, and there is none else, there is no God beside me." I was too busy to give my Father attention that he so rightfully deserved. He had to get my attention; he'd placed me here to serve him and I was doing everything but that.

Over the course of these eight weeks, my prayer life changed significantly. Old habits and the company it kept began to shed like dead skin. A shift was taking place, I felt a renewing in my soul. I looked forward to going to my class every Sunday morning, because before this class, it was 11 o'clock service only and I was out! I would have never thought of taking this class myself. I was content with Sunday morning service only, because I wasn't truly ready to submit myself totally to God at that time in my life… but God is an orchestrator. He used my cousin to get me to go this class to equip & empower me for what I was about to go through. He knew what I needed. I prayed and spent more time with him. My relationship was becoming more intimate with him, I began to cast all my cares upon him and not try to fix them myself to the point of complete exasperation. I looked forward to that private time with God. Even though I'd prayed before, it was different now and I needed it, I needed him. It wasn't intimate before, I wasn't connected! It's so necessary to have quality private time with God as it allows you to hear his voice.

So often we get caught up in the cycle of everyday life and we don't spend quality time with God, we don't read our bibles, therefore we're not being fed. Scripture is vital in effective prayer; it is your armor of protection! Ephesians 6:13, "Therefore put on your full armor of God, so that when evil comes, you may be able to stand your ground, and after you have done everything, to stand." My fire was out, I was merely existing. I had allowed my everyday life to get in the way of my precious time with God. I wasn't reading my bible, I wasn't spending time with him and even though I was going to church, I wasn't living a clean and righteous life for Christ. Even in my unfaithfulness, God was still faithful. He said it in his word that he would NEVER leave me nor forsake me and he has done just what he said he would. He knew I wasn't equipped for the tumultuous events that were going to take place in my life. He continued to orchestrate...

In the midst of me reconnecting with God, I had agreed to meet a friend back in my hometown of Muskegon, Michigan after I had initially said "No". In the reconnection I could hear him better, feel his presence and discern when I was supposed to do something or not do something. That relationship is vital, it saves you from YOU!

I had been seeing my childhood friend (Lady Trina Wells) posting on social media that she had a book collaboration conference for **A Next Level Shift** that was going to be the same exact date that I was going to be flying into town. I thought of course I will go to support her. In fact it would be of total surprise to her since we hadn't seen each other in nearly 20 years. I thought I would get my book signed, see some old friends and keep about my way. Well let me just say, this wasn't your expected book signing loves! Not even hardly! The presence of the Holy Spirit was all over that conference room. Women were being delivered, yokes were broken, there were some speaking in tongues, Prophetic words were being spoken over us & I was slain in the spirit. Yes, slain in the spirit! My spirit had awakened after that night.

As I road back home with my aunt, I kept saying, "What happened in there? I didn't know it was going to be like this!" This was certainly not what I came for. I knew God had his hands on me. The shift had begun in me and I was supposed to be at that conference. There was a prophetic word spoken over my life at that conference and I knew when I returned back to Atlanta, that something was going to happen. The prophet spoke over me as if she had been on her knees next to me listening to me pray to God, it was verbatim... Confirmation! I knew it was confirmation; I never got to spend time with the friend that I flew there to see! God used that friend, a vessel, to get me there for the conference. Quiet yourself loves, so that you can hear his call. For he is God! There's nothing impossible for him!

I knew after that my life would not be the same. I could not run from God any longer. I had to surrender all of me to him. Psalm 119:11, "I have hidden your word in my heart that I may not sin against you." That was how I internalized my relationship with God. I didn't know what was going to happen, but I knew I had to rely on God for whatever it was.

After returning home, I went to my Survival Kit Class and I felt in my heart that my dad was going to die while I was there sitting in the class. I left church, went to my cousin's house and told her just that it was the same cousin who invited me to the Survival Kit Class. She just looked at me and consoled me. As we cried together she asked me all kinds of questions as to why I was saying that and I assured her that I just knew... I knew it, I could feel it in my spirit. That relationship was being nourished. God was preparing me. 1 John 4:13 stated, "This is how we know that we live in him and him in us. He has given us His Spirit." She didn't even finish the class might I add, because the class wasn't for her, it was for me.... God used her to get me there, I know that now.

My dad had been in remission from cancer for two years; he and I spoke over the phone nearly every day. He sounded fine and had assured me he was ok, but he wasn't. The cancer had returned with a vengeance as he had a tumor on his kidneys. He didn't tell me because he knew I would try to do everything I could to take care of him since that's what I did in my profession and he didn't want me to do that. He didn't want me to be his caregiver; he said that first off.

He told me during the beginning of the cancer journey that if the process didn't work of harvesting his bone marrow and transplanting it back into his body, not to press the issue further as far as preventive measures, and that my step mom knew what to do. I was reluctant but, I promised him I wouldn't. It was just hurt so very bad because we hadn't always been so close. The new relationship that we built was beautiful, respectful and honest therefore I had to respect his wishes. He was such a soldier during his fight, but his time had come to retire and rest.

I thank and praise God for the mending of our relationship before he passed away. As we were planning the funeral, I felt that I needed to reach out to my church clergy for support, to pray or speak at his home going service. There again the Lord orchestrated... At the time of his death I encountered a strong praying intercessor that I would have never crossed paths with in the church. I was put in contact with Minister Eleanor, a true woman of God! She has been so very supportive to me since the passing of my dad. The book of Isaiah 41:10 states, "So do not fear, for I am your God. I will strengthen you and help you; I will uphold you with my righteous hand." It amazes me as I look back and see that God was speaking to me through Isaiah as I began to shift and God directed me to Survival Kit Class that was studying the book of Isaiah! My God is awesome!!! You can't tell me that he isn't real! There is none like him!

Had I not been receptive to the invitation to do the Survival Kit Class, I would not have been equipped for that unexpected blow. I really began to sulk after my dad passed. I knew that my path was changed. I began to pray for God to send me some sisters in Christ while I was on my journey; sisters that could teach me how to be a better me...Sisters that I could learn from prayer warriors to pray with and for me. He did just that.

You see, it's a "Shifting" that is taking place so it's a process to this. So he began to eliminate... People that I used to spend lots of time with began to dwindle down to no time spent at all. Not that I didn't love them, but we were no longer on the same paths, so we had to part. I would have stayed stuck, I would not have seen where God was trying to take me, but I had to trust the process. It gets lonely when you begin changing old habits & old friends fade away. You have to stay focused! God knows what he's doing.

As the shift was continuing, I crossed paths while working one day with a new sister that God had blessed me with. At the time I didn't know her, but Tammy was her name. Tammy was actually working with a hospice client of mine and as soon as we began to converse, I knew she was a woman of God. I said "Lord, I see you." Once again, he was orchestrating, directing my path.

Nothing in this life is meant to stay the same. The one thing that you can always count on to happen is change! Change is going to happen whether you want it to or not. How you handle it depends totally upon you. I saw Lady Wells on social media posting about another book collaboration, **A Next Level Shift, Vol. ll.** I watched her for a few weeks inviting, people to contact her and finally I messaged her to inquire about the slots left and she replied, "I was going to ask you Sis." I was numb at the fingertips, because I didn't expect her to say that, yet glad that I was obedient and listened to what my spirit was telling me. I accepted and was humbled to be blessed with such an opportunity.

Ok Lord, now what am I going to write about? I was reminded of the scripture in Isaiah after I asked the question, Isaiah 43:19 states: "See, **I am doing a new thing!** Now it springs up; do you not perceive it? I am making a way in the wilderness and the streams in the wasteland." It was all foreign to me, but I trusted God through it. I knew he wouldn't bring me to it and not bring me through it! He has never ever forsaken me.

I have a prayer partner whom I was blessed to come in contact with through my job as well. She just so happens to be a First Lady and Assistant Pastor of her church, Ms. Charlayne. I call her "Sister Holy Ghost." She has been an intercessor for me in prayer for years. As I was going through the process of writing my chapter, the enemy was busy. You see, it was too much positivity going on in my life. God was working new things in and around me, renewing me… I was "Shifting". The enemy didn't like that! As long as I was in the world living wordly, existing and not living on purpose, he didn't bother me. I was no threat to him because I was dead in the spirit!

You see the "Shifting" began when God used my cousin to get me in the Survival Kit Class. I was existing in the Valley of Dry Bones at the time. Even though I was going to church, that word that was being brought forth wasn't reaching me… I had to have the word spoken directly to me in order for God to reassemble me… I had to have breath enter me! You know the story in Ezekiel 37:4-6 "Then he said to me, Prophesy to these bones and say to them, Dry bones hear the word of the Lord! 5 This is what the Sovereign Lord says to these bones: I will make breath enter you, and you will come to life. 6 I will attach tendons to you and make flesh come upon you and cover you with skin; I will put breath in you, and you will come to life. Then you will know I am Lord." That class strengthened me, strengthened my relationship with God… Began a Shift in me!

God loved me so, that he dispatched his angels all around me. He put people in position for me at the right time in my life. When he knew

I would need them, because he's an on time God! He is the only one that can intricately orchestrate this ensemble. As he was reconstructing me, he was building up my strength to withstand the next trial that I was about to face. The enemy was roaming! He tried to set up shop and take over my son. He tried to break our family bond. Oh yes... he tried it, but he wasn't successful! By that time, my armor was on & my prayer life was strong!!! I had my prayer warriors that God had already orchestrated me to meet, when I was in the Valley of Dry Bones. They were already interceding on my behalf so you see, me and mine were covered! Isaiah 54:17 NKJV states, "No weapon formed against me shall prosper!"

My weapon was sharpened & that was my prayer life! The word of God says in Ephesians 6:17, "And take the helmet of salvation, and the sword of the spirit which is the word of God!" I prayed without ceasing for my child because, I know God had a plan for him. That's why the enemy came after him in the first place. Ephesians 6:12 KJV states, "For we wrestle not against flesh and blood, but against the principalities, and powers, against the rulers of darkness of the world, against the spiritual wickedness in high places."

There was another sister, co-author, Pamela "What What", at **A NEXT LEVEL SHIFT** conference, who happened to have some blessed oil and I got a bottle from her that night. I took that same blessed oil, prayed over my child, over my family, throughout my house over the doors and window sills. I commanded the enemy to leave my home & release my child; he had no authority there. We are God's property! I was on a mission to save my family and the only way that I knew how to do it was to fight with what I had been equipped and empowered with and that loves, was the word of God! I refused to let the enemy have my son that was not happening. I kept praying and I prayed and I prayed some more! It felt like I was praying through a massive rainstorm that slowly began to stop.

I didn't recognize him as my son, when the enemy had latched onto him. He looked the same physically but, spiritually he was missing. God not only answered my prayers to release him from the grips of the enemy, he saved him & filled him with the Holy Spirit too!!! Hallelujah! Glory be to God!!! I just can't thank God enough for everything he has done for him and continues to do. Had I not had be blessed with the spirit of discernment, I would have lost my mind experiencing that. As much as I love my son, God loves him more and I had to let go and trust God to bring us through. What an Awesome God he is!

When you decide to follow Christ, it's not easy. No, it's not, but you have to keep trusting him and stay on the course. You won't ever be ready if you keep telling yourself, "I have to stop doing this or that" making up reasons why you aren't ready & worried about what people are going to say about you. That's a cop out! One of my grandma's favorite sayings was, "They talked about Jesus, what makes you think they won't talk about you, what makes you think you are so special?" I couldn't let procrastination allow me miss what God had for me. I'm growing in him each day, it's a relationship that gets more interesting the more you spend time with him. The sisters I had been praying for, God was sending them to me through this book collaboration and through my church groups. When you trust him, wholeheartedly trust him, your life will begin to transform in ways you never dreamed of.

Through the transformation, I started going out to church conferences on Saturday night with my prayer partner and women's brunch, instead of hanging out and clubbing. Yes God, I see you! July 2017, **A NEXT LEVEL, SHIFT Vol. II** launched in Muskegon Michigan, my hometown. It felt surreal to be a part of something so beautiful. The co-authors were all so beautiful inside and out. Some of them I knew, most I didn't, and they were all kingdom minded women! They all had written personal and very transparent stories that were all so very different, but as I read them I could relate to a part of every story that had been written. Each story had significance, and needed to be shared to help someone else get free from whatever bondage that they had been held in.

I met a co-author that lives here in Atlanta, Denise. Denise and I had never crossed paths and are from the same hometown and now both reside in the same place. How ironic is that? She's an awesome woman of God. We exchanged contacts, and decided to have a book signing in Atlanta to circulate the book. We had one book signing and invited a few ladies to come. My friend Tammy came to this particular signing and come to find out, she is a recorded gospel artist! She had never mentioned to me that she was a singer, but after the book signing Denise said, "Tammy gave me a CD." I said, "What?" Now she had been my friend before the book, before Denise… How did I not know that? God was still orchestrating!

Denise and I had a couple more awesome book signings, inviting our sisters, and it's always seemed to be a different group of ladies, with just a few familiar faces. Each time it was an amazing time in the Lord because the Holy Spirit met us wherever we congregated! We invited the sisters to share their stories as well and it was so good for their souls to just release what they have been holding inside. Late fall 2017 Tammy called me up and said she wanted to have an intimate setting at Denise's clubhouse for New Year's and call it "The Shift". The Shift was infectious!!! It was Amazing! I mean, this girl is anointed and she came to praise God when she picked that mic up! The Holy Spirit was in that clubhouse! This is all being birthed from **A NEXT LEVEL SHIFT**.

Denise then decided for us to do a group that we call "Girl Talk". It's so uplifting and motivating, the ladies that we are coming into contact with are not by chance, it's all of God, he has a word for his daughters, and he is sending hope to them. They need to be encouraged and refreshed and reassembled! He's using us to reach them. Each and every author that has written in these books is a vessel. Isaiah 41:6 states, "They help each other and they say to their companions, Be strong!"

Out of the obedience of Lady Wells and her faith in God, she birthed this! God used her to help his daughters and she was a willing vessel for him. We needed to be free from the bondages that we were in. Through these stories we were able to release the pain, the secrets, confusion and doubt of ourselves that we were living with. My heart is overjoyed every time Denise & I have a "Girls Talk". It never fails that the ladies say, with weeping faces as they thank us and hug tight, "I didn't know it was going to be like this." I say to them, "Love, that's the same thing I said when I went to the first shift!" I truly didn't know. I love sharing with the women I meet and I look forward to having our group, because I know that someone is going to be blessed. I know that this is what God wants me to do. I keep learning as I am being shifted. I am here for my Father's business...The Shift is so Real!

Thank you Lady Wells for your motivation and your courage, you are an Amazing Woman of God. I Love you.

Sherry Johnson

IT'S ME AND MY STORY

Now my story will probably sound like many others who have gone through similar experiences. However, with my story, I am going to give you the process that occurred with the actual events and when they happened. In the year of 1965, I was five years of age and my mom and stepfather moved our family to Cassopolis, Michigan.

At five years old you are in a happy place playing with dolls, playing dress up with your mother's jewelry and walking in her high heel shoes. At this age, your motors skills and other skill sets are just starting to develop. You know right from wrong, but your ability to articulate is vague. You depend upon your parent's guidance, instruction and protection. Typically, this is how things would appear to be in the average household. Yet, I have a different story to tell.

My life changed and was interrupted from being a normal little girl to living in a dysfunctional situation. The events that followed this dysfunction turned my life into a nightmare that began to spiral out of control. I was literally living in hell! It started while my mother was in the hospital delivering one of my siblings. The enemy planted a demonic seed inside my stepfather that made him sexually assault me at my tender age of five.

I didn't know what was happening to me. All I knew was that I was very frightened and wanted my mother to come and help me, but she never did. Each night that my mother was in the hospital, he repeatedly pulled me from my bed and violated me. The cycle occurred over and over again until I reached the age of twelve. I was dying on the inside; all my hopes and dreams were being stolen from me by this violator. I hoped things would change, I prayed things would get better, but it did not.

How do you express yourself, your hurt and pain, to the people who are supposed to protect you, but don't? What do you do when your innocence is stolen from you? How do handle the rage? How do you deal with the scars after the violation? I was left with the broken pieces, the scars that robbed me of my virginity, my pureness, and my childhood.

I remember how he would tell my mother, "Here's some money to go shopping for the kids. I'll babysit while you are gone." This was his way of getting me alone to use me for something I was never created for. I was created to be a winner, but instead the enemy used this man to ruin what God created within me. These demonic acts occurred mostly on the weekends and during summer breaks. I was his "Sex Slave". I knew it was wrong, but I was too afraid and ashamed to tell my mother or anyone else. When he would touch me, all I could do was block it out of my mind.

There is an emotional breakdown that occurs when continuously experiencing rape. All my sense of security was gone. Nightmares and confusion soon followed. This man did not care that I was a baby! He had the spirit of a pedophile.

This is the breakdown and process that took place during the raping as a child:

1. **Fear**. It caused me to feel unsafe, afraid, and also brought about unstableness, insecurities, and lack of trust within myself. To better understand this trial in my life, we'll call it "seeds", and they got planted into my soul as fear entered in.

2. **Identity Theft**. This occurs when the recipient of the rape has been put into slavery in their mind. The enemy causes confusion which covers up and hides who you really are. Now the perception of yourself is distorted.
3. **Renaming Yourself**. At this point in your breakdown, the enemy begins to bully you with words. He uses people to start picking at you. For example, children at school… you become a target. What happens next is the kids at school seem to turn on you with name calling and destroying your character. It puts a burden on your soul. It's a strategy used to cause further breakdown in the loss of your identity. Often this spirit also uses your parents to call you and your sibling's names. This was so bad for me that I couldn't even look at myself in a mirror because I could only see the hideous person that I felt I was.
4. **Physical Bullying**. This occurs when the actual physical violation and contact happens and it caused fear to increase in my life more and more.

As a young girl growing up in this much darkness, it caused me to be the "Black Sheep" of the family. No one wanted to be around me as I was slightly overweight, clumsy, awkward, etc. The most pivotal factor that really damaged me was being overweight. I felt ugly and that's what I believed… until Jesus came in and rescued me. As a result of the name calling, bullying, sexual and physical abuse, however, my life continued to spiral downward for the worse.

By the age of twelve, I was already performing sexual activities with boys and older men. I had developed many additive behaviors like bulimia, pornography, witchcraft, hatred, rebelliousness, unforgiveness, suicide, anger and lying. The arch enemy of my soul tried to destroy me! "Lord, please save me from this destructive lifestyle I am living," I would plead.

As I cried out to God, I could hear the voice of the Holy Spirit saying, "My grace is sufficient for you." I didn't know what that meant so as I kept weeping and wailing day after day, night after night, it seemed as if God wasn't listening to me. "Where are you Father?" I felt completely abandoned.

In my mind I was sinking under the pressure of confusion. I looked for help in those who had been saved a long time, but that didn't ease my pain. Even though I was going through this darkness, I was determined to move forward; then the host of darkness showed up once again and pressed me down even further.

The lying spirits came to reinforce the confusion, telling me I was backslidden and I had committed the unpardonable sin against the Holy Spirit. I really began to search myself at this point. I asked God to show me where I went wrong. Still the heavens were silent to me and with no answer from above, depression began to set in. Now a grown woman, I began to further lose my identity, my marriage was destroyed, I lost my home, my finances had crumbled, my health began to break down, and I began to listen more to the loud voices of the enemy.

They told me I was losing my mind, but I kept saying, "I have the mind of Christ. I have a sound mind." The witches and warlocks had banned together with demons. They jumped me and beat the crap out of me, but I still wasn't giving up! I cried out to God all-the-more and quoted His word back to him. The pressure didn't ease up at all. I am not going to lie; this broke me down to the lowest common denominator. I felt like a fraction being reduced. I had no idea that I was going through the process of the old man being exposed, purged, and put to death so that the new man could arise.

The south side of Chicago is where I was born and raised, but the Lord led me to the state of Mississippi; the Mississippi Delta as a matter of fact. I didn't want to go there, period, however God knew that this was the place he had prepared for me to receive my deliverance. He planted me in a little city called Ruleville and that is where I had my encounter with the Lord Jesus Christ.

For the first time in my life, I had truly experienced real joy and peace. I was on fire and I wanted everybody to know JESUS. A few years had passed and I was still witnessing and lifting up the name of JESUS and going back was not an option. However, nobody informed me that a time of testing was coming and it was designed specifically for me to fail.

THE TEST

We all know that in order to move to the next grade or level you have to take a test and pass it. So the Holy Spirit led me to the book of Psalms 139:1-7. This chapter deals primarily with the omnipresence of God. As God was teaching about whom He really was, darkness came and covered my spirit like a blanket. The light within my inward house went out. I felt that I had been thrust into a cold, dark spiritual dungeon. My first response was once again confusion. Then I began to cry out to God, "Oh Lord, where are you?" I again felt lost and hopeless. I was so scared that I literally shook violently inside.

THE FURNACE

King James Version- 1 Peter 4:12- Beloved, think it not strange concerning the fiery trial which is to try you, as though some strange thing happened unto you:

King James Version- 1 Peter 1:7- That the trial of your faith, being much more precious than of gold that perished, though it be tried with fire, might be found unto praise and honor and glory at the appearing of Jesus Christ:

The furnace is a place used to purify precious metals. I want you to understand that this is a place of intense heat and its purpose is to remove the dross from the precious metals. The refiner will put the metal in the furnace and turn the heat all the way up. He does this in order to start melting the metal and as the metal liquefies, all the impurities begin to come to the top. The refiner then removes the dross that is on the top. He sticks it back into the furnace and will do this until no dross is left. By the time this process completes and all the dross is gone, the refiner can see his reflection. This is what happened to me in the spiritual furnace of God.

Heavenly Father, I Sherry Johnson, your daughter and servant, do thank you for the process of the fiery furnace. Thank you for keeping me even when I tried to run from the heat. Thank you for causing me to understand so that I could stand against all the wiles of the devil and the flesh. I thank you in Jesus' name, Amen.

If you're in the heat of the furnace right now, I encourage you not to give up in your mind and don't faint under pressure. Jesus is with you in the furnace as He was with the three Hebrew boys.

MY FIGHT OF FAITH

When you are going through a trial of such magnitude, the powers of hell encamps around you. They cabal you meaning that they encircle you, hem you up and attack you from an offensive position, in order to bring you onslaught and invasion against you. It is the demonic force's position to bully you into giving up and press you down and press you out. However, the Holy Ghost taught me how to fight back!

He taught me that through the mind of Christ, authority in His name, and prayer that I could send the demons and witches fleeing for cover. I began to push them back with the Word of God. He told me to cover and camouflage myself with the Blood of Jesus, to pray in the Spirit at all times, and fast.

This is how He builds you up to do battle or spiritual warfare. So as I began to obey the instructions of the Holy Ghost, the victory began to come. We are more than conquerors through Jesus Christ. This is how

God helped me in my darkest times to fight back and now I am still moving forward in Christ.

In this training, I was taught to separate faith from feelings. Your feelings will always try to dictate your moves and feelings are connected to flesh. On the other hand, your faith keeps you connected to God, so I literally had to learn to walk by faith.

WHAT DOES IT MEAN TO WALK BY FAITH?

To walk by faith means this: Trusting in God's promises no matter what you are going through; no matter what things look like or feel like. God's promises are what God has said in the Word to the believers. God has a sure promise for you concerning every area of your life. Simply believe and obey the instruments that are written therein. God will give you the victory in everything! This is how God gave me the faith to **"Get My Fight Back"**.

Sherice Dixon

THE FIGHT IS FIXED

The fight is fixed, but most definitely the fight is real; whether the fight is physical, spiritual or emotional. Spiritually we are fighting an invisible force, but the effects of the fight affect us physically and emotionally. The Bible doesn't use the word "fixed" but the Bible tells us that God will fight for us. When referring to the word "fixed" in this context, it means something is predetermined and not subject to or able to be changed. No matter what the fight looks like, it is fixed and can't be changed. He will fight our battles.

In the Bible there are countless times when God tells his people He will fight for them. God is using us in the physical, but spiritually, He is putting us through a process where we can pray to Him, trust Him and depend on Him. Look at Jehoshaphat's prayer to the Lord:

2 Chronicles 20 :12 states : For we have no power against this great multitude that is coming against us; nor do we know what to do, but our eyes are upon You…

Then the Spirit of the Lord came upon Jahaziel… thus says the Lord to you: "Do not be afraid nor dismayed because of the great multitude, for the battle is not yours, but God's…You will not need to fight in this battle. Position yourselves, stand still and see the salvation of the Lord."

The Lord gave three directions to Jehoshaphat.
1. Don't be afraid- No matter what it looks like, I Got this.
2. Position Yourself- Be ready for whatever is coming.
3. Stand still and see the salvation of the Lord- You Win!

Reflect and write down some times when you were in a fight, whether it was spiritual or emotional, and God has fought the battle for you.

_____
_____
_____
_____
_____
_____
_____
_____
_____
_____

THE FIGHT IS REAL

To Fight: To take part in a violent struggle involving the exchange of physical blows or the use of weapons.

Physically we may not experience the blow, but sometimes the fight is so intense, we take a physical blow to our emotions. We are in a fight to keep our mind at peace. We are in a fight to keep our ways and heart pure before God. We fight because everything in us wants to react out of the flesh, but we will never gain understanding in our flesh.

Even if we know that prayer is the way and we know that we are fighting a spiritual battle, living in this realm is difficult when we have been beat down in our emotions. We may not see the fight physically, but spiritually there is a fight in the heavenly realm or world that's taking place. The fight is over DESTINY. YOUR DESTINY! OUR DESTINY!

Ephesians 6:12- For we wrestle not against flesh and blood, but against principalities, against powers, against rulers of the darkness of this world, against spiritual wickedness in high places.

The enemy uses various kinds of weapons against Christ's believers. Weapons of deception, distraction, disappointment, discouragement, depression and so many other things. Guess what? The enemy even uses people against us. So our fight isn't with flesh and blood. The fight isn't about who hurt you or did something to you. Even more so, the fight isn't even about you. The fight is about what you possess on the inside of you.

What are some weapons the enemy uses against you?

_____
_____
_____
_____
_____
_____
_____
_____
_____
_____

Yes, God will fight for us. While God is fighting, let's find ourselves fasting and praying in the process. We have to stand on what we know about God to be true. We have to speak God's truth over our minds. Find scriptures that will encourage us to continue to fight. Here are some scriptures for your reference:

Psalms 27:1-3 states- The Lord is my light and my salvation; whom shall I fear?

Psalms 46:1-3,7,11 states- God is our refuge and strength, a very present help in trouble.

Isaiah 54:17 states- No weapon forged against you will prevail, and you will refute every tongue.

Jeremiah 1:19 states- And they shall fight against you, but they shall not prevail.

Exodus 14:14 states- The Lord will fight for you.

Isaiah 59:19 states- When the enemy comes in like a flood, the Spirit of the Lord will lift a standard against him.

Isaiah 49:25 states- For I will contend with those that contend with you.

Above any of these scriptures, God is a God of war.

There are things we must do in the process while God is at work for us and in us. We must read the Word of God and worship Him to keep our mind at peace. The Bible says those that worship Him must worship Him in spirit and truth. Spiritual fights can't be fought in our emotions. When we choose to handle spiritual fights emotionally, this keeps us frustrated, irritated and it leaves us open to speaking negative things. We open ourselves up for the enemy to place doubt; then here comes the trickery, lies and deception.

Then the battle in your mind will have you on a rollercoaster, trying to figure out what is a lie and what is truth. Unchecked emotions breed confusion. From there, we then begin to question where is God in all of this. Regardless of how the enemy presents the fight to us, be it spiritually or emotionally, the fight still belongs to the Lord.

LEARNING IN THE PROCESS

1 Corinthians 2:14- A carnal mind can't conceive the things of the spirit.

It is hard to see and think things clearly when we are carnal minded and fleshly. It is hard to put things in perspective when the mind is clouded with the negative. It is easier to throw in the towel than to stand in the fight. When we allow the enemy into our space, he will have us to believing we have a right to give up in the fight. He will feed our mind lies. He will have us justifying why we should give up. But thanks be to God that God said we are not ignorant concerning the enemy's devices. These are the kind of lies he feeds us to get us to give up in the process.

What if there is a purpose for the fight? Remember as I stated before, the fight has nothing to do with us, but all about what God is trying to accomplish through us. Though we may not understand, we may hurt, we may cry or even suffer for a while, the fact still remains : it's for the Glory of the Lord.

I even found out that God delights in our brokenness, our hurt and pain. Don't fight against what God is trying to accomplish through your life with murmuring and complaining. There may be times when you want to give up and times when you don't want to fight anymore, but giving up isn't an option.

What if your personal fight was for you to break cycles of defeat in your family? What if you were the one who God needed to rebuild or tear down? You may be fighting for your marriage, family, career or even your identity. Identity, I conclude, isn't an easy fight to win.

Without fighting, you will never grow in strength and you will never know that God will fight for you. However, losing the fight is only conceivable to those who stop fighting. Yes, the fight is fixed but only to those who stay in the fight.

What action plan can you take to stay in the fight?

_____
_____
_____
_____
_____
_____
_____
_____
_____
_____
_____
_____
_____
_____
_____
_____

No matter what, WE WIN!

Kmetris Hunt

LET 'YOU' ARISE

'LET' – Hebrew (Phonetic: haw-yaw) To Be, Become and ARISE.

Too often we live by and or cater to the perceptions, ideas and standards of others rather than those which were predestined by God from the beginning.
   "You can't do that!"
   "You can't go there!"
   "You can't have that!"
We have put our own desires and plans on the shelf and even allowed our circumstances and dilemmas to shape us into someone other than what we were created to be…so much to the point that we don't really know who we are.

Just think about the time someone asked you, "Who are you?" Nine times out of ten, you couldn't tell them who you were. WHY?? Because what WE think of or know about ourselves is usually out of reach and the only way to respond is to rehearse what others have already told us about ourselves.

There is a greater and better you that awaits! A YOU that you have never seen or known. A YOU, you must face in order to overcome!

As often quoted by Poet, Marianne Williamson:

*"Our deepest fear is not that we are inadequate.
Our deepest fear is that we are powerful beyond measure.
It is our light, not our darkness that most frightens us."*

THE DAY 'YOU' DIED

Take a moment and began to think about the person you were at an early stage of life. The time when you had no worries or fears. The time when you were free-spirited and full of life. When you didn't have a care in the world. For most of us, that was the time we were babies or small children. When we trusted without hesitation. When we loved without fear. Have you ever asked yourself, "What ever happened to her or him?"

As I have shared previously in the book, "A NEXT LEVEL SHIFT, Vol. I", I recall being very happy and full of life as a little girl. I remember spending a lot of time with my grandmother while my mom was away in college. She would pray with me every night before bed and that ritual has stayed with me throughout the years.

I remember so vividly the day my grandmother passed away. This was not a good day for me as I screamed and cried so much at her funeral. She was a safe-haven for me, so when she passed, it was as if a part of me had died as well. And I did, because what lied ahead of me, no one had prepared me for, however, God had a plan.

I was about nine years old at this point in my life. All was well, that is, until the sexual and physical abuse began at the age of 10. This was the turning point of my life. The beginning of my innocence being snatched away from me. The moment fear, doubt and distrust entered my heart. I began to ask myself, "Why is this happening to me?"

I can remember the pain and anger I felt on the inside after enduring many years of abuse by the hands of several men in my life. The mental and psychological thoughts about myself began to wear on me. I was ashamed and felt worthless. I began to think that it was my fault and that I deserved it. I lost all awareness of who I use to be and began to submit to the person I was taught to be.

I was no longer the happy, loving and trusting individual. I had become what had happened to me which lead me down a dark path. I didn't know which way to go or who to turn to. I felt abandoned by so many. I had not experienced or felt a healthy sense of love in a very long time. I became bitter, angry, hateful and had a disdain for men. I had died to myself, but God was always there, even when I didn't know Him or feel Him.

The enemy stole from me, tried to kill my dreams and ultimately wanted to destroy me to the point of no return. God wanted a better life for me, and He was now getting ready to show me.

John 10:10 tells us that, *"the thief (the devil) cometh not, but for to steal, and to kill, and to destroy: I (Jesus) am come that they might have life, and that they might have it more abundantly."*

'YOU' THOUGHT IT WAS OVER

I am now 18 years old with two children out of wedlock, when God sends a young woman to minister to me and invite me to her church. After much hesitation, I finally got the nerve to go with her and receive salvation. This was the greatest experience of my life. Now mind you, I had been to church before as a little girl, but nothing like this. I experienced God's power and His presence for the first time in my life.

All was well until I began to see something familiar trying to attach itself to me. Something I knew all too well and now I was seeing it in the church. Yes, I said it, in the CHURCH! ARE YOU KIDDING ME??!!!

I would sense a strong spirit of perversion and manipulation whenever I was around certain individuals. And because I had experienced it so much in my childhood, that spirit continued to seek me out.

Often in life when we come into a new place, there are things in our past that will try to come along as well. The bible says, *"That if any man be in Christ, old things are passed away, and behold all things are new."* But it appeared that the same demons I was fighting before salvation were still there after salvation. Some of the things I had experienced with people outside of the church began to happen inside of the church. It was almost like there was a sign on my forehead inviting these spirits into my space.

Naturally, because I had been familiar with manipulation, misuse and dysfunction for so long, I figured it was normal. It was easy to live this life. So I continued even in the church year after year living a life that I couldn't seem to get away from. I even got married at the age of 19, but that spirit kept on following me. I didn't know how to fix it. No one had taught me how to get free. The more I tried to run from or change things in my life, the more I seemed to do them. I felt like Paul in the book of Romans 7:19-24…

"19 For the good that I will to do, I do not do; but the evil I will not to do, that I practice. 20 Now if I do what I will not to do, it is no longer I who do it, but sin that dwells in me. 21 I find then a law, that evil is present with me, the one who wills to do good. 22 For I delight in the law of God according to the inward man. 23 But I see another law in my members, warring against the law of my mind, and bringing me into captivity to the law of sin which is in my members. 24 O wretched man that I am! Who will deliver me from this body of death? 25 I thank God—through Jesus Christ our Lord!"

'YOU' ARE NOT WHAT HAPPENED TO 'YOU'

In life we will experience some things that will affect us positively and or negatively. These experiences usually dictate the type of influence it will have on our future self. Because of the many years of heartache and pain I had endured, I became someone I didn't even recognize or liked. I had allowed what had happened to me to enter my heart, therefore becoming bitter and cold. I would lash out on others because of my own pain. I had become one with my pain.

This reminds me of the woman with the spirit of infirmity for 18 years in Luke 13:11. The bible says she was bowed over and could in no wise lift herself up. She had been influenced and paralyzed by her circumstance to the point where she could not pull herself up out of her dilemma. That was me!!!

I remember being so thin because I had no appetite to eat because of depression. But even through all of that, I still wanted God so badly. I wanted to know Him and feel His presence after being ostracized and abandoned by so many. When it was all said and done, it was just me and God. I had no one else to lean on nor call on at this point. I didn't want to give of myself to anyone, and I didn't want anyone trying to love me.

As I fell down on my knees in the middle of my living room floor, I began to cry out to God for help. After being labeled and told I wasn't chosen, all I could do was weep before God.

There's a phrase we often used as kids that says, "Sticks and stones may break my bones, but words will never hurt me." Well, that isn't so true…words do hurt and can also have an effect on you mentally depending on what is said and who is saying it. However, God began to tell me His thoughts towards me, which were of peace and not of evil to give me an expected end (Jeremiah 29:11). He told me how much He loves me and how He wanted me and that I had put my trust in people, more than in Him. He had chosen me, and no one could take that from me. When I heard that, I began to rejoice and picked myself up off the floor. It is God who validates us, not man. Now it was time to fight for her!

'YOU' Have to Surrender

Ok, so how do you fight for something when you are unsure of who you are and the life you are supposed to live. What I soon found out was that I could not fix or change myself within my own strength. I needed a power and strength far above mine. The strength that the bible speaks of in 2 Corinthians 12:8 which says, "And he said unto me, my grace is sufficient for thee: for my strength is made perfect in weakness." This was the beginning of me relying and leaning on God for strength.

God began showing me that in order for me to reclaim my life, I had to surrender it to someone who would love me better than I could ever love myself. Jesus said in Matthew 10:39, *"He that findeth his life shall lose it: and he that loseth his life for my sake shall find it."* Sounds like an oxymoron, right? You mean I have to give up my life in order to get it back? That didn't sound like a good plan seeing as a lot of my life had already been taken from me.

So, how could I trust this Jesus when I didn't know Him? How am I to know that He won't disappoint me like all the others? The bible lets us know in John 3:16 that God loved us so, that He gave His only son for us. Well I didn't recognize this kind of love because I wasn't familiar with someone sacrificing their life for me. The thing that stood out most was that Jesus was a "GIVER". I was used to people taking from me, not giving.

So first, God had to deal with my mind, because it is with the mind that we serve the Lord. He had to strip me from my pattern of thinking and the words that had been spoken over me by others and even by myself. Philippians 2:5 states, *"Let this mind be in you, which was also in Christ Jesus."* There was a mental battle going on that I had to overcome before I could ever overcome spiritually or naturally. Romans 12:2 states, *"And be not conformed to this world: but be ye transformed by the renewing of your mind, that ye may prove what is that good, and acceptable, and perfect, will of God."* My mind needed to be transformed. This was going to take work was a process.

The mental breakdowns that happen to us just don't happen overnight, but they happen over a period of time; and so will your healing and deliverance. So, as I began to delve greater into the Word of God and meditate on it day and night, change began to take place. It took me speaking over my own life, what God said about me.

Jeremiah 2:21 says, *"Yet I had planted thee a noble vine, wholly a right seed: how then art thou turned into the degenerate plant of a strange **vine** unto me?"* See, when God planted us, He created us noble and whole. We were honorable in our own right, established, and true to ourselves. We were created without dysfunction, however because of the fall of man, we were shaped into iniquity and conceived into sin; thereby causing us to sometimes not live the abundant life set before us.

TAKING 'YOU' BACK

It's okay to love you and be there for you. As women we often give so much of ourselves to everybody else, thereby losing who we are in the process. Recently, I began to look at how I had catered to so many others to the point I didn't even know what I liked to do.

It had gotten so bad that I was literally burned out, overwhelmed with trying to make stuff happen for others, and I wasn't taking care of me. It was now time to enjoy life. I even had a tough time buying something for myself because I was used to putting others before me, but this was getting ready to change. God taught me how to say 'NO' in some certain areas of my life where it seemed people only wanted to take and not reciprocate.

Yes, I'm still a giver, but not to the point of burning myself out. So, I began to tap into the noble, whole person God originally created me to be and began to fight for that person. The real 'ME' that was underneath everything that I had experienced. The 'ME' who God had created and predestined before the foundation of the world. The loving 'ME'! The kind 'ME'! The giving 'ME'! The creative 'ME'! The 'FREE ME'!!! **I FOUGHT, AND I WON!!!**

Who has God called you to BE? I commission you to tap into that person and fight for her. Not the person that others have labeled you as. Not the person of your circumstance. Not the person of what happened to you in your past. Not the person that the world has conformed you to, but the Real 'YOU'. Our Abba and Father created us with dominion, power and authority. There's a greater 'YOU' that awaits. A 'YOU' without limitation. A 'YOU' without fear. A 'YOU' with genius ability. Tap into the 'AUTHENTIC YOU and Let 'YOU' ARISE!!!

"LET 'YOU' ARISE!!!

Pamela Buford

GIRL, GET YOUR FIGHT BACK POEM COLLECTION

Girl Get Your Fight Back means different things to different people. One of the ways I got my fight back was allowing poetry writing to become a positive healthy outlet for me. Here are a select few I would like to share. I call this my How I Got Over Collection.

I pray it blesses you.

Evangelist Pamela WhattWhatt

I AM A POET

The words came knocking at the door of my heart with a shout
I did not seek them out
The words have something they wanna say
My job as a Poet
Not to get in the words way
The words have seen things
The words have heard things
The words have experienced things
They wish they had not
The words have a mind and a will of their own
The words can not be stopped
The words are my friends
They allow me expression of things too wonderful, too marvelous, too painful to suppress within
The words have something they MUST say
My job as a Poet ..
Not to get in the words way
The words care about me and you
The words are not through
I Am A Poet

"WHEN YOU SPEAK'
John 10:27 GW
My sheep respond to my voice, and I know who they are.
They follow me

As long as I can Hear You when you speak
that's really all I need
if my heart is bleeding...

Trina D. Wells

Or Maybe I'm just feeling needy
Something's happenings
And I begin to sway
Demands of the day
Be it as it will or may
Situations pulling me every which way
As long as I can hear you when you speak
I won't sink
Into the quicksand
Of the demands
Of others
That try and smother out my light
If I can hear your voice in the midst of it all
I'm Alright!!
As long as I can hear your voice
I can stay the appointed course
Being in the secret place is totally up to me
See
I choose to stay in position
Where My heart meets the condition
To receive
The nuggets you send
Thru the tests of time
I might bend
But never ever break
For Your sake
I proceed
You fulfill my needs...
When People hurt or offend
Deep oh so very deep within...
I can't afford to go into a tailspin...
I simply decree and declare the victory

I still win….
Because the real battle is within...
As long as I can hear your voice
I know I'll always make the right choice
In every endeavor
I'll never
Not need to hear from You
Every dark night that I make it through
I Give All the Glory to You
I can't make it without You
I wouldn't even want to
The sound of your voice is soothing music to my fears as well as my ears
It Calms my savage beast
Penetrating places no one else can reach
I march on
To the beat
Of your drum
No matter how hum drum
life might feel at times
I shine
I rejoice
When I hear your voice
I rejoice
I dance In the rain of anointed by fire
I don't tire
I rise above and beyond everything that I aspire..
I sing
your voice is everything
It enables
Keeps me stable
As You prepare my table
Your voice encourages me

To
Stay in the press
I say Yes
I believe every word I hear
I sense the very near
Ness of You
It takes me through
It all
Thou times I stumble
I don't fall
I listen, await your call
Like a woman madly in love
I rise above
Emotional degradation , depression , and shame
Your voice
Is reliable
I'm viable
Again
Valuable
Voluptuous
Waiting in anticipation
Of our next encounter
I counter balance
I overcome heart wrenching pain
Because your voice
Reigns supreme
In my ear
I hear
You
As long as I can hear your voice
I breathe where the air is thin
Where there are very few friends

There you pay a dear price to attend
I function
I blend in
I don't have to people please
To be welcome or at ease
As long as I can hear you when you speak
I'm strong not weak
Week after week after week
We meet
You greet
Me with such warm and enthusiasm
I experiencing spiritual orgasm after orgasm
Yes this is really happening
Because I can hear you when you speak
When you call
I drop it all
And come running
Cause when enemies are gunning
In my direction
You alone are my undefeated protection
Thank You for reaching out to me
Thank you for coming in my direction
……………………..As Long as I can hear you when you Speak

"FACE IT"
John 8:36 KJV
If the Son therefore shall make you free, ye shall be free indeed.

I face my today
Knowing it will not magically rearrange, disappear or go away
I take a look inside my soul's every room
I spoon
Feed my space
To another place
But it still leaves the same trace
That leads
Right back to where I plead
With God to deliver me from
So today I come
Bringing no pretense
No fence
To separate farce
From reality
I see
My reality
I am alone
At home
Have been for much more than a while
Thou I smile
And make the best of it all
I don't fall
Apart
I start
A new life for myself
Except

It feels like something is missing
Deep down inside I'm wishing
God would come and rescue me
From my reality
It hurts
And what's even worse
It feels void of true meaning
Oh sure there's you God
I love You with all my heart
After You
There's a few
Far and in between family and friends
But that's where it pretty much ends
I'm free to come and go as I please
God has blessed me to have all I need
I'm not between a rock and a hard place
I don't have a bitter taste
Towards anything or anyone
That is a waste of my precious time
I don't waste my dime
On meaningless conversation
My only reservation
Is that my self preservation
Is wearing thin and out
To God I shout
Out loud
Dear Lord I'm crying inside
I can no longer hide
The impact my reality creates
Oh God I'm oozing with heartache
With way too much Me time
I find

Myself
Wishing
Missing
Being connected
I'm feeling rejected
Unprotected
Unloved or cared for
I see the door
That stands between
Myself, my past and my future
However
Painful
The Endeavor
I'll never
Return to the past
I'll last
Because I know At long, long last
My God Given
Moments will appear
I have no fear
The sheer
Anticipation
Creates lighthearted elation
As I prayerfully wait
My pain dissipates
It's healthy to express
The mess
I was from time to time
I find it therapeutic
Now everything is lining up like a rubric
Cube
I believe

It's not too late
I await destiny's call
I don't fall
Apart
I continue to start
A new life for myself....
.

"THE STILLNESS"
Psalm 46:10 KJV

Be still, and know that I am God: I will be exalted among the heathen, I will be exalted in the earth.

There something in the stillness
Something we mustn't miss
It's sweeter than your first kiss
Essential to your progression
Let me make this confession
I didn't want it
But it haunted
Me
Until I obeyed its instructions
Little did I know it was an induction
Into a realm in the spirit
There you can hear it
All so clear
Your fear
Will disappear

Jesus is so very near
You can touch His garment
There is no harm in it
There's something in the stillness
You need
You won't find it in any book you read
You have to relax and wait
It just like a date
With the person you love most
The Holy Ghost
Comes and soothes
That bad mood
You try and disguise from others
In the stillness you can uncover
all your flaws
The things that creepy crawl
Around in your heart, soul and head
When you lie in bed
And you can't really sleep
It's ok to wail and weep
At His feet
Let His word become the meat
That meets all your needs
Allow Him to tell you
How, when and where to take heed
Gives validating instructions
On how to pursue your dreams
It seems
Unreal
But in your heart it feels
Just right
You're no longer uptight

You gain insight
The stillness brings all you need
 to succeed
Now you can confidently proceed
There's something in the stillness
There's something in the stillness
We need ...
Please take heed
There's something in the stillness
There's something in the stillness
We need ...
Please take heed
There's something in the stillness
There's something in the stillness
We need ...
Please take heed

"YESTERDAY I CRIED"
Psalm 56:8
New Living Translation

You keep track of all my sorrows. You have collected all my tears in your bottle. You have recorded each one in your book.

Yesterday I cried
didn't try to hold it inside
I put aside foolish pride
And plain old-fashioned cried
I didn't try to hold it inside
Though it took me by surprise
The source from which the pain came
it was a shame

But not my shame
you see I've openly borne
the blame of my shame
So I don't have to play that game…
No more so
yesterday when I cried, and oh how I cried
Inside I felt a release
A sense of peace
Although my peace came at a very dear price
I freely paid that price
to avoid my spirit turning to ice
I refuse to throw knives
Become one who connives
Full of bitter resentment
Sorry not sorry
I sent that invitation away
Sorry not sorry
I'm not available that day
I'd rather pray the pain away
Than to react that way
Yesterday I cried and it cleansed away the painfully inflicted pain
I gained
A new vantage point
A view of something new
I don't have to do
What you did to me
To make it through
Yesterday I cried and I'm cleansed
Yesterday I cried and Heaven became unhedged
Because I didn't pretend
Yesterday I cried and heaven defends
Yesterday I cried and heaven makes amends

Yesterday I cried and heaven attends
to my tears
Yesterday I cried and heaven calms my fears
Yesterday I cried and heaven holds my hand.
Yesterday I cried and heaven understands
Yesterday I cried and heaven commands
my day
Yesterday I cried and heaven makes a way
For me...for me ...for me
Because Yesterday I cried
Because Yesterday I cried
Because Yesterday I cried

"SHE ARE"
Psalm 139:14 KJV

I will praise thee; for I am fearfully and wonderfully made: marvellous are thy works; and that my soul knoweth right well.

Observed like art
Studied from afar
They run by foot
Drive by car
They Speculate
They implicate,
Some even try and duplicate
But they can't
Cause
She Are
She Are
She Are
That Star

That shines
Even blinds
The eye
They shy away
They can't stay
The light blinds their eyes
They can't conceive in their minds
The depths of whom
She Are
She Are
She Are
That Star
That Shines
Even Blinds
In daylight
Don't play like
You can't tell
You smell her delight
You feel her pain at night
You see her battle scars
She Are
She Are
She Are
Authentic
She in it
For the long haul
She accepted the call
Yes she fall
But She bounced back to win
From beginning to end
She all in
She Are

She Are
She Are
That star that shines
Even blinds
In the winter time
She walk in sunshine
God said She mine
All the time
Even when She whine
She mine
All the time
I keep her mind
When y'all ain't got time
To recognize her brilliance
Or appreciate her resilience
When y'all treat her like she a million miles away
God said
I spend the day with her on Mother's Day, Her Birthday, Valentine's Day, Thanksgiving Day, and Easter Sunday
When y'all don't even say
Hey
Have a nice day
God say
At Christmas Time
She Are Mine
We sing and dance
I give her a present
Of my presence
Its seventh heaven
She Are
She Are
She Are

That Star
She sets the bar
For others
Pain can't smother
Out Her genius
She Are
She Are
She Are
That Star
That shines
All the time
Even when she can find
A friend
She win
By default
Cause it's not her fault
She gives till it hurts
Though enemies lurk
That can't destroy her product
God got her
She Are
She Are
She Are
That Star
That Shines
God said
She Mine
She All Mine
All the time
She Are
She Are
She Are

That Star
That Shines
Fall, Winter, Spring,
Summer Time
She Are
She Are
She Are

#WhattWhatt

"LET IT RUN ITS COURSE"
Psalm 27:14 KJV
Wait on the Lord : be of good courage, and he shall strengthen thine heart: wait, I say, on the Lord

Let it run its course
Don't force yourself
Torture yourself
Because you still feel
Just be real
Time will heal
Your heart
Don't start faking and pretending
Wait for an authentic new beginning
That will create an ending
The Pain will stop
You won't have to hop
on one feet
Say three Hail Mary"s
Dance to the beat

Of your favorite song
Relief will come along
In its time
Try not to whine
Or feel sorry for yourself
Acknowledge your pain
Don't pretend that it has left
If it's still there
Take care
Become proactive
Instead of retroactive
Don't wait
Until it's too late
Don't depreciate in value
Have strategies in your pocket
When pain trys to sock it
To you
This is what you do
ABC
123
Pain you can't overtake me
I won't deny your existence
But you can't dominate or become co- existent
Be persistent
In your prayers
Cast your cares
Where they belong
Go home
Face your fears
Cry if needed
Then dry your tears
Communicate with your innermost being

It will jumpstart you into seeing
Life in a healthier perspective
Accept redirection
Get where you need to be
On the path to destiny
Let it run its course
I promise you
No remorse
Of course
It all up to you
To be true

To You
And see it through
Just Let It Run Its Course
#GGYFB

Trina D. Wells

Made in the USA
Monee, IL
02 April 2024